RECOVERING FROM DEPRESSION

A companion guide for Christians

Katharine Smith

First published in Great Britain in 2014

Society for Promoting Christian Knowledge
36 Causton Street
London SW1P 4ST
www.spckpublishing.co.uk

British Library Cataloguing-in-Publication Data
A catalogue record for this book is available from the British Library

ISBN 978–0–281–07075–6
eBook ISBN 978–0–281–07076–3

Typeset by Graphicraft Limited, Hong Kong
First printed in Great Britain by Ashford Colour Press
Subsequently digitally printed in Great Britain

eBook by Graphicraft Limited, Hong Kong

Produced on paper from sustainable forests

To my husband Adrian,
who with steadfast love and patience
continues to be my closest companion
and my best friend.
Thank you

Contents

———•═•═•———

Contents

Part 4
ALPHA AND OMEGA

Part 5
JOYS AND SORROWS

Foreword

This is a resurrection book. As Christians, we know that, through his death and resurrection, God in Christ has achieved everything necessary for our salvation. The New Testament piles up image after image to help us understand what has been done for us, but at the heart of each one is God's complete victory over all the things that hold us captive or separate us from God and from each other.

It may not seem obvious why God's victory can only be won through Jesus' willingness to undergo suffering and death, but Paul says, in Romans 8.38, that it is so that nothing can 'separate us from the love of God in Christ Jesus'. Christ Jesus has taken the faithful love of God into the darkest places of human experience, so that God's life can be found even there.

When Jesus is raised from the dead, the scars of his suffering are still visible: he is not remade so as to wipe away all memory of what has happened to him. But his resurrection demonstrates that suffering does not have the last word; it is not the final truth: the life of God is the ultimate reality. So Jesus was able to go to his disciples, those who had run away and left him to die, and offer them another ending to the story. He offered them the chance to renew a relationship that they thought had been killed and, as in so doing, their past became the life-giving good news that they were then able to share with others. Jesus is alive! The past cannot be rewritten but it can be redeemed and become fruitful.

And that is why Katharine Smith's book about depression is a resurrection book. It does not try to wipe out or deny the reality of the suffering that she has undergone, but to offer it as a story that testifies to life, to good news.

Katharine's book is a mixture of different kinds of writing. It contains practical advice, about when you really need to go to A&E and what will happen when you do; or how helpful antidepressants can be. It offers journal entries from times when Katharine was wrestling with depression herself; it has stories, based in reality, that explore what the deep roots of depression might be, so that we can begin to be truthfully loving and healing towards ourselves. It also offers psalms, biblical passages, liturgy and poetry.

The book does not need to be read at one sitting, and it will certainly be a book that people come back to over and over again, at different stages of depression or caring for people suffering from depression. Different passages will leap off the page at different times, in the depth, or on the slow road to recovery, or when fearing that the disease is returning. The honesty of this book will make it a trustworthy companion, a hand to hold onto, the voice of a calm guide.

Katharine's earlier book on depression, *Angels in the Wilderness* (Redemptorist Publications, 2010), was warmly reviewed and appreciated but, more importantly, many people who themselves suffered from depression, or lived with beloved companions who did, wrote to say how significant the book had been for them. In particular, many of them said that it was a book that they could give to well-meaning but misguided Christians who told people that they should not be depressed, or that they should be able to pray themselves out of it. This second volume will fulfil a similar function and take it further. Depression is not sinful; it is a disease. Fellow Christians can help by praying, by not being afraid, and by accepting the different stages of this disease and working with them.

After the crucifixion, the disciples were bereaved, afraid and ashamed. When the risen Jesus came and stood among his disciples, he said to them, 'Do not be afraid.' Jesus made a way for the presence of God through all the dark and lonely places of the world, so that nowhere, and no experience, need be cut off from the hope of resurrection. The life of God is eternal; everything else passes, including depression. And this is the truth that Katharine's book echoes: do not be afraid, transformation and new life are possible and hope is more truthful than despair. Katharine is able to speak these words of hope with an authenticity based in her own experience, so that every page is a breath of life, and a promise of resurrection.

Jane Williams
St Mellitus College

Acknowledgements

———•◆•———

I'm very grateful to all the people who have supported me with love and prayer while I've been writing this book, and I'd also like to thank those who have shared with me some of their experiences of suffering from depression and recovering from that illness. Names have been changed to protect individuals.

Thank you to those who have regularly attended Morning Prayer at St Andrew's Church, Taunton since 1999, when I started turning up. I am especially grateful to Julian Smith and Jeremy Harvey, whose Christ-like ministry to me brought hope and healing in some very dark times and whose continuing friendship I value more than they can know. A big thank you too to Robin Lodge, Mike Chapman and Janet Fulljames for their prayerful support and encouragement.

Jane Williams has helped and encouraged me enormously in my writing ministry and particularly in the writing and publication of *Angels in the Wilderness: Hope and healing in depression*. Thank you, Jane.

Sue Latimer has been a very good friend and critic. She has worked her way through this book chunk by chunk, and her comments, questions and suggestions have been invaluable. Thank you, Sue, for hours spent putting the world (and the Church) to rights, and for sharing with me your wisdom, insights and incomparable sense of humour!

And, finally, thank you to Alison Barr and everyone at SPCK for making this book happen!

Prologue:
A meditation on approaching Easter

―・◆・―

Morning has broken like the first morning.
And as on that first morning,
light blazes out into a new world,
driving back the darkness and chaos,
rolling away the stone of death.
And the darkness and death will never overcome
this new light and life of resurrection.

Blackbird has spoken like the first bird.
And somehow all the birds of the air
know with their very being
that this dawn is like no other.
They greet it with a joy that tears
at the hearts of the women who weep.

How can another day dawn like this?
How can the sun shine with such brilliance?

But at least this morning they have something to do.

They were helpless
as they watched their friend, their Lord, tortured to death on
    a cross.
They were helpless
as they watched his body being placed in the tomb.
They were helpless
as they endured the long hours of the Sabbath day.
But now, at last, early in the morning
they can do something.

They can reclaim his body
from callous soldiers and jeering crowds.
They can honour him

with tender washing, spices and perfume.
They can say goodbye with privacy and dignity.

After that . . . who knows?
Somehow their lives will go on
but how empty and desolate they will be.

But then, in the early morning light with the sound of exultant
   birdsong
above and around them, they know that something is different.
They know it at that deepness of the heart which is rarely mistaken.
Something is different;
the stone is rolled away from the entrance to the tomb.

But it's not just that – there is something else,
something more other-worldly and mysterious.

They're not sure whether to dry their tears
or weep with some new and terrible sorrow.

What can there be to hope for and yet . . . and yet.

Dare to draw near, you women who loved Jesus,
and take us with you into the mouth of the tomb
where the sun's light will never reach.

Let us dare to draw near with them.
Let us dare to go forward
from the fear, dread and despair of our Gethsemanes
from the shame and agony of our Golgathas
with our scars and damaged hearts.

Because if we do draw near
we too will see the young man in his white robe,
holding his hand out to us in love and friendship,
hear him say,

'You are looking for Jesus of Nazareth, who was crucified.
He has been raised; he is not here.'
'Jesus of Nazareth has been raised;
he is not here.'

It's the dawn of a new day, a new age.

How often do we hang on to the guilt and shame
which we brought with us from the Garden of Eden?

How often do we remain captive
in the dark Garden of Gethsemane?

How often do we allow ourselves to be joyful
in this Garden of Resurrection
and the new life that is ours if we will only believe?

'Morning has broken like the first morning;
blackbird has spoken like the first bird.
Praise with elation, praise ev'ry morning,
God's re-creation of the new day.'

Alleluia, Christ is risen,
He is risen indeed, Alleluia.

Part 1
INTRODUCTION

1

Days of resurrection

———◆•●•◆———

Easter Day begins in darkness. It begins with the grief and fear, loneliness and despair of two women, Mary Magdalene and Mary, the mother of James. They think they have lost everything that gave their lives meaning and direction. They feel the darkness in their world cannot get any darker and the pain in their souls cannot get any sharper. They don't yet know what has already happened: it happened while they were mourning and during their deepest anguish.

Silently and secretly the first whispers of a new dawning have begun to spread through creation and are about to reach the hearts of the two women called Mary.

Easter Day begins in the darkness of Good Friday and the shadow of the cross.

Living through the darkness and shadows of depression can feel like living through our own personal experiences of the Garden of Gethsemane and Golgotha. We may know anxiety, fear and dread of what tomorrow might bring. We may have a sense of having been let down and betrayed by people we thought of as friends. What is happening to us is unjust and cruel. We look at the devastation of our lives and feel utterly abandoned and forsaken by God.

It can seem as if Easter Day will never dawn for us and we are condemned to live this half-life for ever without understanding why. We might ask, 'What did I ever do that was so bad that I deserve to be punished in this way?'

The answer to that question is, of course, nothing. Depression is an illness that suffocates many, many people, and being a Christian certainly doesn't make us immune to it. It's a terrible thing to live with, terrible both for the person involved and for the people who love and care for him or her, but it's never something we 'deserve' to suffer or a punishment of some kind.

I suggested above that Easter Day begins in the dark and with weeping. I believe that, in the same way, recovery from depression begins when we first become aware that something has gone very wrong with the way we're thinking, feeling and behaving. We realize that we are not ourselves, and that others are concerned about us. From that time of recognition we make a start on our pilgrimage of recovery. It probably won't feel like that, though! Life will probably seem very dark and scary. Sometimes it's true that our world is at its darkest just before dawn – but the dawn is on its way.

Easter Day will dawn for each of us and this book is about the pilgrimage from our Gethsemane and Golgotha to our Easter Garden. It comes from my own experience of recovering from depression and walking in the light once more.

I am now a licensed Reader in the Church of England and work as a freelance writer. I have no academic qualifications in either psychiatry or psychology and I am not a trained psychotherapist or counsellor. I have, though, experienced episodes of depression throughout my adult life and probably in childhood as well. This has had a profound impact on every aspect of my life, and especially on my work, on relationships with colleagues and friends and on my journey of faith.

I've read many books about depression, its causes and treatment, and delved into a lot of self-help books on various aspects of personal growth and relationships. I've also often engaged in short and longer terms of counselling and psychotherapy. In 2010 my book *Angels in the Wilderness: Hope and healing in depression* was published by Redemptorist Publications. In that book I tried to describe something of my struggle with depression and how it related to my Christian faith, using stories of healing encounters with Jesus described in St Mark's Gospel.

That book ended with a chapter about resurrection and the beginning of recovery from depression. It introduced some of the themes I'll be developing in this book, which I hope may be a companion to people who have left the darkest days of depression behind them but are aware that the process of recovery and growth continues throughout our lives.

My last major episode of depression began somewhere in the first months of 1999, when I became too ill to work. About a year later I started working part-time for a different organization, but in March 2001 I spent three weeks as a voluntary inpatient in a psychiatric unit. It took another two or three years for me to get to the stage where I could 'manage' my condition and not feel totally overwhelmed and unable to live any sort of 'normal' life.

During this time in the dark valley of shadows I received effective medical care and therapeutic support from a consultant psychiatrist and my GP, both of whom gave me hope that I would get better and encouraged me on my way there. Friends at my church held me in love and prayer with patience and understanding even when I was particularly difficult to be around. Above all, my beloved husband Adrian loved me, cared for me and put up with my misery, selfishness, anger and all the other horrible and negative stuff that was flying around us, sapping our energy and motivation.

After several years of recovery and much reflection on the whole experience, I think I've come to an understanding of what was going on for me, what helped and, although I still sometimes get lost and confused, how to prevent any more major episodes.

My experiences won't be the same as anyone else's. Each of us is a unique individual living in different circumstances and with different stories to tell. Because of that truth I can offer no straightforward answers or easy-to-follow directions. What I can offer are insights I have gained, lessons I've learnt by trial and error along the way and words that continue to give me comfort and strength and an ever-growing faith that:

> All shall be well
> and all shall be well –
> and thou shalt see it thyself
> that all manner of things shall be well.
> (Julian of Norwich)

It may be that you are suffering from depression yourself or perhaps you have a concern for someone going through that experience. Whoever you are, I hope that you will find something in these pages that resonates with your experience, offers you encouragement and helps you somehow to feel that even in the times when you feel most lonely, in fact especially in those times, you are never completely alone in that loneliness. God is there; he is with you and he is on your side!

2

What are we recovering from?

One of the most surprising things for me about recovering from depression is that for a lot of the time I can't actually remember just how dreadful it was to be under such a dark and heavy cloud. It is, of course, wonderful and hugely encouraging to have lost that sense of hopelessness. But sometimes I do need to remember that I have been very ill in the past and that I am still vulnerable in certain circumstances.

I would encourage everyone on this pilgrimage of recovery to bear in the back of your mind what it is you've been through and how this may affect your life now, especially in the early days of recovery. Sometimes it can be helpful to hold our experience beside the experience of someone who has had a serious injury or a physical illness rather than a mental one. Doing this can shed light on the ways in which depression may continue to shape our lives and how best to manage it so as to prevent it getting a tight grip on us again. I'll be saying more about this later on.

For now let's just remind ourselves of some of the debilitating symptoms of depression and how these may have affected or disrupted our lives. Not everyone will have experienced all these symptoms but I suspect that most will recognize the majority of them!

- Our mood was very low or flat. We weren't able to enjoy things like we used to, laugh at comedy, get excited by an action film or care who won a sporting tournament. There was no joy, no warmth, no anticipation and no sense of purpose.
- Although we seemed to lose the ability to experience positive moods and emotions, negative ones remained and may have been very powerful: anger, fear, grief and any number of other destructive feelings may have been crowding our minds.

- Our sleep patterns were disrupted. We'd get to sleep quite quickly (maybe helped by medication) but we'd wake up early, somewhere around 4 a.m., and be unable to get back to sleep, our minds filled with negative and self-destructive thoughts.
- Anxiety and particularly low moods were often at their worst when we woke up and would completely overwhelm us before we had a chance to resist.
- Our eating habits were also disrupted. We might have stopped eating healthily and either lost weight or gained it by 'comfort eating'.
- We couldn't concentrate on anything like newspapers, books or television programmes. This might have made it even harder to make decisions and choices on comparatively minor day-to-day things like what to wear or whether to have a bath or a shower!
- Our self-confidence was shredded and we felt useless and bereft of our usual skills. This, combined with a sense of isolation and disconnectedness, made it very hard to socialize. We might have cut ourselves off from other people, even good friends.
- We were (and might still be) taking medication which itself can cause uncomfortable and unwanted side effects.

Any one of these symptoms would have been bad enough on its own. Experiencing all or most of them at the same time was overwhelming.

From her own experience of depression J. K. Rowling created hideous beings called 'Dementors' and describes them like this:

> Dementors are among the foulest creatures that walk this earth. They infest the darkest filthiest places, they glory in decay and despair, they drain peace, hope and happiness out of the air around them. Even Muggles feel their presence, though they can't see them. Get too near a Dementor and every good feeling, every happy memory, will be sucked out of you. If it can, the Dementor will feed on you long enough to reduce you to something like itself – soulless and evil. You'll be left with nothing but the worst experiences of your life.[1]

Imagine we had had a physical illness or disorder that had caused this level of disruption in our lives and made it impossible for us to function normally or at all. Imagine such a physical illness lasting for eight months, a year, 18 months. In those circumstances we would understand why our recovery took a long time and why we needed continuing treatment and careful readjustment in order to resume our lives.

I hope that thinking like this may help us all to have the same level of understanding and patience about our own recovery from depression. It might also help those close to us to understand why we're not able to 'get back to normal' quickly and why we may need to make some big changes to cope with long-term effects of this invisible illness.

I'm not sure why it's often so difficult for us and others to accept these ideas. Maybe at some level we never really accepted we had a recognized illness that needed medical intervention. Maybe we consider ourselves weak and pathetic when we struggle to do things we used to manage without any difficulty at all.

Whatever the reason, it doesn't help our recovery if we feel that everything 'wrong' should become 'right' again very quickly and by our own efforts.

However, it's also unlikely that time and/or medication alone will bring about a full recovery without any effort on our part. We do need to work at recovery but we need to work with, not against, our own God-given being. It seems to me that many people who suffer from depression find it very hard to treat themselves gently and with great care. But self-bullying and putting a lot of pressure on ourselves will be counter-productive. We need to be compassionate, gentle, patient and encouraging towards ourselves.

So far we've talked about recovery from the clinical illness of depression with its debilitating symptoms and the damage they can do in our lives. There may also be some underlying problems that led to the depression in the first place. Some may say that becoming deeply depressed is actually the first step in recovering from those problems and difficulties. Our minds, our emotions and our spirits are all giving us the message that something in our lives needs a radical change for our own good. Maybe we already knew that, but only paid attention to that need when we were forced to by the meltdown that is depression.

That's certainly how it was for me at the beginning of 1999.

I was working as a legal secretary but no longer enjoying my job. Unable to find another post, I agreed to study for further qualifications which I hoped would improve matters for me. This meant, of course, that as well as working full time and having commitments in my church life, I was studying in the evenings and at weekends.

My mother had died the previous year in somewhat traumatic circumstances. My father had died four years earlier, but I think it was only after my mother died that I was able to grieve properly for both of them.

I was struggling with unresolved emotional difficulties going back to my childhood which, in spite of a lot of counselling over the years, still bothered me and tended to complicate many of my relationships with others and with God.

I was in the second term of training to be a Reader and my spiritual life was taking all sorts of uncomfortable twists and turns that demanded my attention!

It was a time of change and upheaval, and looking back I can understand why depression took such a strong hold on me.

So, depression may be masking many layers of emotional pain. If that is so, recovery will mean treatment for depression *and* therapeutic support so that these other issues can also be resolved or managed in a less destructive way.

Those who have known the shadow of depression and its destructive force often recognize in each other the marks of the illness and the struggle to be free and well.

But we are not the only ones whose lives have been turned upside down by mental distress and who face the challenge of recovery from that pain. All sorts of things can seriously upset the balance of our lives, plunging us into unfamiliar territory and threatening the security of our bodies, minds and spirits: we may suffer a bereavement, a serious illness or injury. An important and long-term relationship may break up, or we might face redundancy and financial difficulties which might also arise from other circumstances. Our lives might be scarred by addictions or violence.

I hope that what I write here may speak not only to people who, like me, are suffering and recovering from depression but also to others who have been battered and bruised in mind and spirit by life's darkness and shadows.

Recovery from such bruising is a lifelong pilgrimage towards wholeness. Fellowship with other pilgrims can in itself bring healing, as we reassure each other that we are not alone in our loneliness and that God is with us and within us always.

3

Where are we going?

My husband, Adrian, and I were spending a day in Venice, a city we love and visit as often as we can. If you have ever been there you will understand how easy it is to lose your bearings and sense of direction as you wander along all the *calles* and over the many bridges that give Venice its extraordinary atmosphere and beauty. On this particular day we had agreed, or thought we had agreed, which of our favourite restaurants we would visit at lunchtime. As we made our way towards food, drink and rest for our feet we had a few disagreements as to directions until it finally dawned on us that we had actually been thinking of two different restaurants in different parts of the city. We would never have got to either of them!

Before we set out on a journey we need to have a fairly clear idea of where we're hoping to get to and be realistic about what that will mean for us as we travel along the way.

When it comes to recovering from depression it may seem obvious that we would want our journey to lead to healing and wellness of our minds and spirits which have been so badly crushed. But we might want to spend some time reflecting on what that word 'recovery' means for us – what it is and what it isn't.

Here are my thoughts on this:

Recovery doesn't happen overnight. It's unpredictable, and our progress, if we detect any at all, can seem slow and involve a lot of hard work. This may well challenge our faith in God so that we want to, or do, cry out, 'How long, O Lord, how long?' We get the impression from Gospel stories that, when Jesus heals someone, that healing is immediate and complete. Why can it not be like that for us? How urgent and desperate must our prayers be before he listens and heals us? Maybe he wants us to be ill or doesn't care. Is he punishing us for something we didn't know we'd done? Is it our fault because our faith is inadequate? Do we deserve to be ill?

Surely the truth is that God longs for us to be well. He may long for it even more than we do ourselves! He certainly knows us better than we know ourselves. But it's hard to believe that truth during our Good Friday. It's then that we need others to believe it for us and to pray for us for the dawning of our Easter Day.

Recovery doesn't mean that life goes back to how it was before. For some of us the event or events that triggered an episode of depression may mean that it's impossible for our lives to return to the same 'normality' we used to know. For example:

- We might be facing our future without someone special and precious to us.
- When a long-term relationship is broken, our view of life and the way we relate to others may undergo a radical change.
- If we have been 'made redundant' (and how degrading and depressing those two words sound) we may need to think about changing direction, retraining or self-employment.

If we'd had a serious physical illness or injury we may have had to adapt to a significantly different lifestyle. The same principle applies when we suffer a serious mental illness. We may have to learn to adjust and to accept new limitations in what we can cope with physically and mentally in order to prevent further episodes happening.

Even if there have not been such clear 'triggers' for depression we may have a sense that something within us has broken and can't be completely mended. Our perceptions and priorities may have shifted, causing us to rethink all aspects of our lives.

And our lives will have new markers: 'Before', 'During' and 'After' the Darkness. But these are not separate distinct stages. Before, During and After will blend together to become our present reality. It is in that new, yet ever changing, reality that we will need to learn to live.

As we grow, recover and change we will probably find that our relationships will need to change as well. This may not be easy for those around us to understand. They may not know what it is to face an unknown future and to feel as if we're standing on shifting ground, only just keeping our balance. Their everyday lives may not have been significantly altered by our illness, bereavement or other difficulty, and as their lives continue as normal we may feel left behind, isolated and lonely.

Recovery is a long-term process, and depression can keep us in its grip for a very long time. This again may be very hard for others to understand. An episode of depression can go on for weeks, months or even years and it may well be impossible for some people to maintain the level of support they were able to offer at first. The withdrawal of support and help is not an intentional unkindness although it might feel like that. Our friends who know something about this experience will be aware that we need their continuing understanding and patience. But it can be painful to feel that others expect us to have 'got over' the illness long before we have recovered any stability in our lives. Worse still is the unspoken message given by others that we are in some way responsible for the depression continuing and we need to 'snap out of it' or 'pull ourselves together'.

For me, recovering from depression means that we experience a lightening of most of the debilitating symptoms we looked at earlier. We sense the internal changing of the seasons and the possibility of resurrection. We learn to trust our improved moods and outlook on the future. We enjoy life again, and in fact may feel happier and more able to cope with 'normal' demands much better than we ever did. We've reached the point where we can 'manage' our condition, and we'll be looking at how we ourselves can prevent further episodes of depression later in this book.

Recovery is not a final destination. I don't believe that in this life any of us reach complete healing and wholeness. I do believe that recovering from depression is an ongoing process with ups and downs, disappointments and hopes, grieving and celebration. Like everyone else, we continue to learn and to grow in maturity as we become more like the people God means us to be, but that pilgrimage of faith reaches its fulfilment and perfection only when, through God's grace, we enter into his eternal presence of love.

4

The process of recovery

The early days

What happens when a man suffers a heart attack while at work, or a girl is knocked off her bike as she cycles to college?

Probably someone will call the emergency services and paramedics will be sent out followed by an ambulance. There will be an assessment of each situation and, if needed, treatment will be given before the ambulance can take the patient to hospital.

Once in A&E there will be further assessment, monitoring and treatment until the patient is able to return home or is transferred on to a ward.

Most people can understand and appreciate these early stages of treatment and recovery after an illness or injury. It makes sense to find out causes, assess the damage done and to plan a course of short-term treatment. I think it's much harder for people to understand that the same sort of process goes on for those with clinical depression or other mental distress.

With depression there might not be any obvious cause of a crisis. One morning, after struggling for months to cope, I was quite suddenly and completely overwhelmed, knocked down, by feelings of exhaustion, anxiety, despair and dread. I can't even remember what the 'final straw' was but it plunged me into a horrible darkness from which I could see no escape.

My husband, Adrian, made the emergency call to our GP's surgery asking for an appointment that day. The immediate treatment was medication and being 'signed off' from work for a prolonged period.

There followed several months which I now think of as my time in 'A&E' and intensive care: a time when I was hanging on by my fingertips, barely able to cope. I was at home rather than in hospital, but ordinary things like taking a shower, getting dressed and doing the smallest bit of housework took me a long, long time and used up what little energy I had.

In these early days of recovery I struggled to get through each day, to make a phone call, to go to the doctor's surgery or to do some ironing. Sometimes it was a major achievement just to struggle from bed to sofa! It was too frightening to look ahead, yet my mind conjured up terrible thoughts about what the future might hold. Very often I just didn't care about anything; I just wanted it all to stop. I slept a lot, cried a lot, ate a lot, raged a lot and beat myself up for being so horrible, pathetic and useless. These experiences may sound familiar to others who have been diagnosed with depression.

Sometimes it's very hard to pinpoint a decisive moment when our lives turned upside down, inside out and back to front and we were left feeling disoriented and a stranger to ourselves.

In the same way it can be hard to pinpoint a decisive moment when the symptoms of depression begin to loosen their grip on our minds, but somehow it does happen. The spinning slows down, we feel more steady and we catch a glimpse of direction and purpose in life. We sense a lightening of our darkness and an easing of the burden we carry. The early days of crisis and helplessness are passing. We're moving forward to the next stage of our pilgrimage along the road of recovery.

The long and winding road

Let's go back for a moment to think a little more about the man and the girl we met at the beginning of this chapter. They were both taken to A&E for emergency treatment; the man because he'd had a heart attack and the girl because she was quite seriously injured when she was knocked off her bike.

The immediate initial treatment and care has been given and they are both now ready to look ahead and think about whether or not they need to make adjustments, big or small, to the way they live their lives.

He is advised that he needs a healthier diet, to lose some weight and to take a little more gentle exercise. He will continue to need certain medication for the rest of his life.

She will need physiotherapy for her leg for some time, and because her wrist was fractured she may find that she can no longer play tennis at the level that has taken her to the finals of a county championship.

Both of them, in different ways and to different degrees, have had their lives changed. They won't be the same again but that doesn't have to be a disaster. It may well be that from their experiences their lives will be enriched in ways they could not have foreseen.

I'm convinced that men and women who have suffered clinical depression and high levels of anxiety experience similar change and growth as they follow the long and winding road of recovery.

During the early days of my own recovery I was taking medication, both antidepressants and a fairly mild dose of tranquillizers. I was taking enforced time out from work and study, with all the stress and anxiety they had been causing me.

Very, very gradually and with the support of friends and their prayers, the worst symptoms of depression began to ease. The anxiety, distress, hopelessness, exhaustion and weakness became slightly less over-whelming. A realization began to dawn on me that I might now have some choices and decisions to make about my future, even if 'the future' was, for now, only the next two days.

This turning point (or phase might be a better word) unfolded over weeks and months. Experience tells me that very little in recovery happens quickly, although sometimes we can have 'penny-dropping' moments when we suddenly know a new truth or gain a new per-spective which changes how we see ourselves, other people and our relationships.

Most of the time we seem to travel painfully and slowly. We make progress but then fall back. In our minds we keep revisiting places many times as we go round and round in a loop that seems to trap us into repeating the same mistakes and getting hurt by the same situations time and time again. But later the road of recovery becomes more like a spiral. We continue to revisit those places but it's always at a different level with a different perspective, and we make progress in freeing ourselves from the traps.

During this phase of recovery we move beyond that earlier sense of helplessness and weakness. We begin to see hope and a rainbow ahead of us. We are ready to step out and start walking with a sense of purpose.

The hidden things

In Chapter 2 we thought about how there may be several issues contributing to an episode of clinical depression. There may be many layers of emotional pain which are being held deep within us, pushed down out of sight and out of mind by the suffocating weight of depression.

As medication, rest and other changes begin to ease the symptoms of depression it may be easier to identify and think about what might have been contributing to its development. This is like the stage when the man who had a heart attack may be helped to think about his lifestyle and physical health, and how he might change these things to make the best recovery possible and to prevent further attacks.

So, for example, if we have been working extremely long hours under a lot of pressure we may be encouraged to rethink our working life, to make time for relaxation and doing things we want to do with people we want to be with.

Perhaps we have been consciously or unconsciously bottling up a lot of scary emotions. If this is the case then the easing of the symptoms of the resultant depression may mean that all those other emotions, including fear, anger and guilt, start pushing themselves up to the surface of our consciousness and make their presence felt in ways that hadn't been possible before.

At this stage we may experience some confusion about the cause of our negative feelings and thought processes. Do we feel anger as one of the symptoms of depression, or is it one of the long-term effects of an earlier trauma which we haven't yet addressed? Has depression given rise to our lack of sense of self-worth, maybe even self-hatred, or were we harmed in some way in our childhood which has left us with very low self-esteem? And so we could continue listing symptoms that are common to clinical depression and to an earlier experience of trauma, such as the harming of our minds, bodies or spirits in childhood.

It may not be possible to make these distinctions clearly and indeed it may not be necessary to do so. It is important, though, to recognize that they may be there, and to explore that possibility with a professional therapist trained and experienced in this field. Sometimes, of course, it may already be known and clear that some sort of trauma or abuse lies in someone's recent or distant past. But even then we cannot be sure that that is what has caused so much emotional pain that our minds have hidden the feelings away from us for our own protection.

Whatever is going on for us now, we probably feel very exposed and vulnerable. I remember realizing that all my ways of coping with depression and powerful negative thoughts and emotions were no longer effective. But I had yet to find and develop new ways of being to replace the old. Everything in my mind, heart and spirit seemed to be out of my control, unpredictable, messy and frightening.

I also remember realizing that there was no way of going back to before the Darkness. I could only go forward into an unknown and therefore frightening future.

We are extremely fragile and vulnerable in this place. Our emotions are close to the surface and very raw. If the foundations of these emotions were laid in early childhood we may well feel (and behave!) like a young child totally overwhelmed by his feelings and unable to understand what's happening to him.

It's extremely hard for someone who has not been through this kind of experience themselves, or witnessed it in others, to understand the extent of the devastation caused by this 'meltdown' of the mind. For this reason I think it's very important for us to receive long-term therapeutic support from a professional who is trained and experienced in treating patients with this level of mental distress and disorder. It is a huge relief to be able to talk about frightening thoughts and feelings with someone who is not themselves frightened by them but who can reassure us and help us find our way through the chaos and into a new, differently ordered way of living.

5

Where is God?

———◆■◆———

Saying 'yes' to God

So far we've been thinking about recovery from clinical depression and the healing of the wounds that might lie behind the depression. With the right medical treatment and therapeutic support we are setting out on the road of recovery. But before we begin exploring that road further I'd like to spend some time considering how our Christian faith and these experiences might affect each other, for better or for worse.

I remember one particular Sunday morning when our curate preached an excellent sermon about saying 'yes' to God. Her words were challenging and also inspiring and her message was exciting. I could register all those things in my mind but emotionally I felt hugely upset, full of self-doubt and rejected and abandoned by God. How many times during my life had I said 'yes' to what I believed to be God's calling?

I had grown up in a clergy family and attended a Church of England grammar school. I was confirmed and took communion regularly at church and school. I'd assimilated a great deal of knowledge about Bible stories and the major players in those stories. I was familiar with different liturgies, prayers and hymns. Since the age of about 17 I had been searching for a more 'felt' and personal relationship with God. I had repeatedly asked him to let me know his presence with me and was sorry, in a way, that I couldn't be re-baptized so that I could say 'yes' to God in a different way, speaking for myself.

All that praying, all that searching, all that willingness to say 'yes', and what had I got in return? Nothing. Or at least that's how I felt on that Sunday. I felt angry that God apparently didn't want me and didn't love me and totally devastated by what I saw as broken promises and almost a betrayal of my faith, which had clearly been totally inadequate.

Yet I had gone forward for Reader training and had been accepted – what was that about? I was very confused!

My spiritual journey and search for God has been so central to my life from my earliest years that it cannot be separated from my psychological and emotional development and the various problems I had with that.

These experiences may be familiar to others who will understand how complicated our minds are; how difficult it is to rethink our faith in the darkness of depression and how new knowledge about ourselves rocks our sense of self-identity.

Looking back I can see God's hand in so many things that have happened in my life. I can see him working through people who did support me and in circumstances where I felt totally alone and afraid and, sometimes, in real danger. I still find it impossible to understand why it is that when we most need reassurance of his loving presence God doesn't seem to be anywhere near us. But maybe it works the other way round. It's when we lack any sense of God's presence that we feel so alone and desolate: frightened children lost and separated from a loving parent who is frantically looking for them to bring them to safety.

Ministry of friends

As Christians suffering from depression and working through some difficult emotional 'stuff' we need other Christian friends around who can minister to us as Christ would. We are greatly blessed if we have a small group of such people who are as Christ to us, and we need God's grace to accept their ministry.

These are not Christians who say things like:

- 'We have prayed for your healing and you haven't healed straight away. That must be because of your lack of faith – it's your fault.'
- 'If you're not recovering after prayer for healing you may have demons that need to be cast out.'
- 'You should be happy and thankful. Think what Jesus has suffered for you and be grateful and joyful.'

I'm afraid that on one particularly distressing occasion I responded to that last one by saying heatedly that Jesus was on the cross for a few hours. I'd been suffering from all this mental pain for many years!

These responses to our pain and distress are unhelpful, to say the least, and can, as I know all too well, cause hurt and damage which only adds to our already dangerously heavy burden of guilt, fear, shame and suppressed anger.

Loving, supportive and sensitive Christians will show by the way they love and care for us what God's love and care is like.

They are patient and willing to listen to us, saying the same things again and again.

They are gentle and kind in a way that soothes our troubled minds.

They assure us time and again that we are precious to God who loves us and they treat us lovingly because we are so important to God.

They allow us, indeed encourage us, to lean on their faith and prayers when we lose hold of our own.

They forgive us when we lash out at them, understanding that it's often the people closest to us that we hurt the most.

They minister sacraments to us, anointing us with oil or sharing a Eucharist for healing.

They give of themselves in ways that are costly, and remain committed throughout the lengthy journey of our recovery.

And when we are able to live free from the overwhelming pain and darkness they will rejoice with us and for us – an experience that can be powerful and bring further healing in itself.

Ministry of the Word

For some time before I became too ill to work in the spring of 1999, I had been attending Morning Prayer, along with others who were to become so important to me over the months that followed. The prayer and fellowship of this time proved to be a good start to my working day spent in the legal world of wills and probate!

When I was signed off work because of depression and anxiety I tried to continue going to Morning Prayer.

I think just about everyone who has gone through clinical depression will know that mornings are particularly difficult to cope with. Sometimes it's impossible to get out of bed, so heavy and suffocating is the blanket of despair and dread that throws itself over us as soon as we wake up. So there were many mornings when I just couldn't face the day.

But at other times it was good for me to have a sort of commitment to meet at a set time with a group of people to which I belonged and who missed me if I wasn't there. Even if I collapsed in a pathetic heap on the sofa watching television for the rest of the day, at least I'd showered, got dressed and made contact with God by being with his people.

As time went by, some of the words and phrases, canticles and psalms forming parts of the Order of Service for Morning Prayer throughout the year became familiar and important to me. They seemed like lifelines, sometimes expressing my own dark feelings, sometimes offering hope and encouragement, and sometimes lifting my thoughts up to a completely different dimension where the hurt and distress of my life were no more. I'd catch a glimpse of an eternal reality which I might, some time, come to know more fully.

The same was true of many of the Bible readings, which would often set me off on a train of thought about what they might mean for me that day, week or month. Sometimes very familiar passages took on new meanings for me and gave me new insights into what it is to be a disciple of Christ 2,000 years after the first disciples set off on their journey with him.

Pictures of God

Whoever we are and whatever experiences we've known, as we grow in faith so we would hope to learn more and more about who God is and what he is like in his relationship with us.

And herein may lie a significant difficulty for some of us. We may have grown up with, or been taught, ideas of a God who is anything but loving and forgiving. Our experiences of harmful relationships in childhood may make it difficult for us to understand what it is to be completely loved as God loves us or to be forgiven when we think we have totally messed things up.

Even without a problematic childhood, when we are depressed we may find it very hard to believe anything good about ourselves or that anyone could possibly love us or even want us around. We might think that in some way we are 'unclean' and contaminating – a harmful presence when with others.

The negativity of depression is hard to break down; sometimes anything we try to do to counter it just makes things worse, and if you've ever tried to make constructive suggestions to a depressed friend you will probably recognize the 'yes, but . . .' response. 'Yes, but that won't work . . .', 'Yes, but I have no friends . . .', 'Yes, but I'm useless', 'Yes, but I can't', and so it goes on. It's almost as if we can't bring ourselves to try anything, to be willing to follow the advice of others, to risk further disappointment when we don't immediately get better.

God may well have his work cut out to get through these defences we've put up around us and to show us the truth about himself through the words of Scripture, his Word made flesh in Jesus and the ministry of loving friends shown to us as we struggle.

As I continued showing up for Morning Prayer I noticed how often there are reminders to us of the love and goodness of God. Incidentally I also noticed that most of these, and certainly the ones that I still particularly treasure, come from the Hebrew Scriptures (I often reflect on that insight but that's a whole other book!).

At the end of this chapter there are some of the words I have found especially helpful, encouraging, inviting, reassuring or full of promise, words that still speak to me of a God far more compassionate and forgiving than I had imagined.

Struggling with God

When I look back over those years when everything was so difficult and I was so unhappy and afraid, I see the whole experience as one long struggle to free myself from my past and from old ways of thinking and being that were no longer adequate or helpful.

I feel as if, like Jacob at the Jabbok river (Gen. 32.22–31), I was wrestling in the darkness that seemed unending against an unknown adversary who was almost too strong for me. I know that like Jacob I sustained injuries in the struggle which cannot be completely healed. Like Jacob I needed to know what or who it was I was fighting and to reach some kind of resolution to our battle. I sense that I am coming out of that struggle with a new identity, just as Jacob did when his name was changed to Israel because he had 'striven with God and with humans, and (had) prevailed'.

I believe that all of us have our own struggles with God, but also that, even if it is with a limp or scarring from the fight, we can and will walk into the dawning of a new day with our new identity and our new relationship with him.

Readings for reflection

Here are the short passages from Scripture referred to in this chapter. I invite you to read them through slowly, and if one phrase resonates with your need stay with it; just hold it quietly and don't try to analyse it. Allow it to start going deeper into your thoughts, asking God to reveal more of himself to you in ways you will be able to understand. Be very gentle with yourself. Spend as little or as much time as you feel able to cope with. Sometimes God can say as much to us in one minute as he can in one hour! Don't try to make yourself feel different, think differently or be different just because you've read those particular words.

If you are still quite depressed, having a not so good day or are tired, it might be difficult for you to be calm and quiet. Your mind might be too agitated or mangled to process any thoughts in a helpful way. At these times it really is important that you don't drive yourself further into the ground by putting unnecessary pressure on your already beleaguered brain.

One more comment on these phrases: God is referred to as a male in these passages, which can be a very real problem for some people. For others it can be extremely difficult to think of God as female and as a 'Mother'. We can't get round this difficulty easily but I want to acknowledge the pain it can cause some of us and to say that I hope and pray that part of our recovery will be the healing of the hurt that lies beneath the surface of our hearts and minds.

> For the Lord is gracious; his steadfast love is everlasting,
> and his faithfulness endures from generation to generation.
> (Psalm 100.4, *CWDP*, p. 796)

> For as the heavens are high above the earth,
> so great is his mercy upon those who fear him.

> As far as the east is from the west,
> so far has he set our sins from us.
> (Psalm 103.11–12, *CWDP*, p. 800)

> Here is my servant, whom I uphold,
> my chosen, in whom my soul delights;
> . . . a bruised reed he will not break,
> and a dimly burning wick he will not quench.
> (Isa. 42.1a, 3a)

Strengthen the weary hands,
and make firm the feeble knees.

Say to the anxious, 'Be strong, fear not,
your God is coming with judgement,
coming with judgement to save you.'
('A Song of the Wilderness' 3–4, *CWDP*, p. 580)

Full of compassion and mercy and love
is God, the Most High, the Almighty.
(Refrain, 'The Song of Manasseh', *CWDP*, p. 605)

The Lord is my light and my salvation;
whom then shall I fear?
The Lord is the strength of my life;
of whom then shall I be afraid?

Wait for the Lord;
be strong and he shall comfort your heart;
wait patiently for the Lord.
(Psalm 27.1, 17, *CWDP*, pp. 684, 685)

Fear not, for I have redeemed you.
I have called you by name; you are mine.
When you pass through the waters, I will be with you.
When you walk through fire, you shall not be burned.
(Morning prayer for Thursday:
Responsory from Isaiah 43, *CWDP*, p. 164)

Part 2

SETTING OUT ON THE JOURNEY

6

Some essentials

———◆—◆—◆———

Foundation stones

When you have weathered the storm of an episode of depression one thing is certain: you will want never to have to go through another. You will want to do everything you possibly can to avoid that valley of dark shadows and stay in the light that is at last driving those shadows and the fear from your mind.

I wish I could offer you a map and straightforward directions showing a clear route along the road of recovery. The truth is that there are as many routes and pathways as there are travellers, and each of us has to find our own way.

But we might all walk through similar landscapes, face similar challenges and struggle with similar difficulties and threats to the peace and health of our minds. If this is the case then I hope that in describing some of my experiences and passing on lessons I'm learning along the way I will be writing something that speaks to you and maybe supports you along your path. I'm sure that if we ever were to meet, you would be able to do the same for me.

There are one or two foundation stones I would encourage you to put down for your path of recovery.

The first is your determination to avoid at all costs a return journey into your particular Darkness. But you will need more than the desire not to follow that downward path again. You will need determination and motivation to make positive choices and to follow positive and healthy ways of living as you reach out for recovery for your bruised and battered mind.

Your mental health and stability must be your 'treasure hidden in a field' (Matt. 13.44) or your 'pearl of great value' (Matt. 13.45). They need to be so important and necessary to you that, like the treasure finder and the merchant, you will be prepared to do whatever it takes to lay hold of them and keep them.

Does that sound selfish or self-centred? Perhaps it does, but I know for myself that I cannot serve God in the way I believe he has called me to serve him when my mind is preoccupied by its pain and I'm having difficulty coping with ordinary day-to-day living.

The second foundation stone I would suggest is this: the belief that while we all need God's grace and healing in our lives we also need to take responsibility for our part in the process of recovery. Medication may ease the symptoms of depression and a time of rest may loosen the tight knots of stress. What medication can't do is resolve the various problems, issues and lifestyle choices that contributed to an episode of depression in the first place. While these remain at large and untamed they will continue to cause trouble and may trigger further episodes of depression.

Identifying, understanding and finding some sort of resolution of these difficulties within ourselves may be a long-term and painful process. We may need the help and support of a psychotherapist or counsellor, and in some cases this can be arranged through a GP or consultant psychiatrist.

The third element of our foundation is a resolution to be kind to ourselves, to nurture the seed of recovery that was first planted in us when we said 'yes' to the question, 'Do you want to be made well?' Like the mustard seed Jesus talks about (Matt. 13.31–32), the seed of recovery may be very small indeed, barely noticeable, but when planted in the right soil and nurtured it grows and grows until it reaches our whole being, bringing healing for ourselves and hospitality for others.

Choice

'Do you want to be made well?' (John 5.6).

'Of course I do,' we say, amazed that anyone could ask such a question. Who would want to be left in such distress, ill health and isolation? Of course we want to be made well, preferably straight away without our having to do anything for ourselves.

But let's look a bit more closely at this question: it may not be quite as simple and straightforward as it first seemed.

The question Jesus asks comes from a story told in chapter 5 of St John's Gospel (verses 2–9). It seems that there was a popular belief or legend that an angel of the Lord would come down from time to time and stir up the waters of a pool known as Beth-zatha in Jerusalem. It was said that the first person to step in the pool after this stirring would be healed of whatever ailment afflicted him or her.

So, many invalids would spend time beside the pool, watching and waiting for the signs of stirring in the water. Among those invalids is a man who has been ill for 38 years. We don't know what's wrong with him, although it clearly affects his mobility, or whether he's been waiting by the pool for all those years.

When Jesus asks him, 'Do you want to be made well?' he doesn't actually answer the question directly. Instead he explains that he's never managed to get into the water because he has no one to help him.

If we pause at this point in the story we can reflect on how it might be compared with our stories of needing to be made well from depression and other mental distress.

These are my reflections, which may resonate with those of others but we will each have individual thoughts and ideas drawn from our own experiences.

It doesn't sound as if this man has very much hope of ever being the first one in the pool after it's been stirred up. We hear nothing about him asking for help; presumably all the others who are by the pool are either invalids themselves or accompanying relatives or friends, and they will assist them rather than the man. So why does he stay, with no prospect of healing?

Perhaps he has given up any real hope of a cure but is resigned to staying where he is. He's used to this place and knows the people around him, has nowhere else to go and nothing else to do. It would actually be quite scary to try and find other places to be, other people to meet, other activities that he might just manage.

And what if he was healed? He might be dependent on others for his livelihood at the moment. How would he earn money if he could work? His days are mapped out for him; what would it be like to have to make decisions about what he does each day? What would it be like to have to take responsibility for his own life, not to be a victim of ill health or injury?

Although he may not realize it, perhaps he's thinking to himself, 'I'm used to my life, it's safe and predictable, I know who I am and the people I meet. I'm actually quite comfortable here and it's not often the water gets stirred up anyway.'

I've spent some time with this story because I've come to believe that actually we do need to make a clear decision that we want to be made well. During the 'A&E' days we thought about earlier, our pain, distress, anxiety and fear are so high that we're desperate for them all to be eased and are in no doubt of our need for healing. But sometimes when the crisis stage ebbs away we might be tempted to ignore all the longer-term implications of our experience or feel too daunted by the difficulties we'd face if we started dealing with them.

After the man in our story has explained to Jesus why he can't get into the pool to be made well, Jesus says, 'Stand up, take your mat and walk.' And the man does just that. I can picture Jesus holding out his hand to help the man stand up and the man reaching up to grasp the hand of Jesus – his 'yes' to the question, 'Do you want to be made well?' I like to imagine Jesus holding out his scarred hand to help me stand up and move forward, and me grasping his hand – my 'yes' to his gift of new life offered in love.

Commitment

> God of our salvation,
> help us to turn away from those habits
> which harm our bodies
> and poison our minds
> and to choose again your gift of life,
> revealed to us in Jesus Christ our Lord.
> (Additional Collect for Fifth
> Sunday before Lent)[2]

Our decision to choose life, to choose to become well, is unlikely to be a 'one-off' decision. On the road of recovery, as in all aspects of our lives, we will know moments of doubt, weakness, indecision and failure. We may not always realize that we have left the road of recovery and need to get back on to it. We may not have heard the voice of our internal satnav saying, 'Turn around when possible'!

This Collect has become special to me because it expresses so well what I want to pray when I've forgotten or neglected to choose life-giving ways over harmful ways.

Experience has taught me that very often we can't do the 'right' or 'good' things until we've stopped doing the 'wrong' or 'bad' things.

And very often the 'harmful' things we are doing are those that harm ourselves in some way. They may harm others as well, but here we are thinking about our own bodies and minds first.

Only we ourselves know what habits we have that 'harm our bodies and poison our minds'. There are many possible ones:

Overeating	Watching mindless television programmes
Smoking	Playing mind-numbing computer games
Taking illegal drugs	Dwelling on past hurts
Drinking too much alcohol	Gossiping or being judgemental
Risky driving	Nursing a grudge
Lack of exercise	Self-harming

These are just a few – we will all have some we could do without!

Turning away from these may simply require a bit more self-control and restraint, but there may be some that we can turn away from only with professional help. Addictions, self-harming and eating disorders and other harmful ways of being have complex causes and need careful professional treatment.

Deciding that with God's help we will turn away from destructive habits is in itself part of choosing life. It's repentance – turning round to face the right direction. But there's so much more to choosing life than that. We need to make healthy, loving, joyful and creative choices so that we may have the gift of life in all its abundance that Jesus offers.

And when we think about some of the life-giving choices we may want or need to make along the road of recovery, let's remember that our commitment to making these choices may need regular reviewing and renewing!

Don't look back!

> Remember not the former things,
> nor consider the things of old.
>
> Behold, I am doing a new thing;
> now it springs forth, do you not perceive it?
>
> I will make a way in the wilderness
> and rivers in the desert.
>
> ('A Song of the New Creation',
> *CWDP*, p. 293)

31

There is nothing wrong with thinking or talking about the past. What matters is the way in which we think or talk about it, and what we choose to do as a response to past events.

Let's think about how we might look at an album of photographs of a family wedding that took place some years ago. We share with each other happy memories of the service, the reception, the fun and all those people who attended. We look at our friends and family with love and, of course, a touch of sadness for people who have since died. And then we put the album away, with renewed pleasure that it's there whenever we want to see it again or show it to anyone else.

Is that how we look at the past? Or do we look at it like this:

We remind ourselves of all the things that went wrong (even if there were very few and they did no harm), and the things we wish had been done differently. We criticize once again one or two unwisely chosen outfits. We have another pick at the scars of old grudges that we like to keep hold of and nurse. We sigh about how quickly time passes and how old we are now. Then we put the album away feeling grumpy, disappointed in life and as if somehow we've been hard done by, and everyone else probably feels thoroughly miserable as well!

Well, that may be a caricature but most of us, if we're honest, can probably recognize those traits in ourselves at times.

Remembering the former things and considering the things of old in a healthy way may be a necessary part of our recovery. Looking back may help us to understand how people and events have shaped our lives, making us who we are today.

As we reach that deeper understanding we might be able to make peace with a past that has haunted and damaged us. We can learn from all our experiences and the mistakes we've made so that we can reshape patterns of thought and behaviour that have caused us pain and distress.

If harmful experiences in our childhood have contributed to our depression (whether we remember them in detail or not) we will probably need to think and talk about them so that they loosen their harmful grip on us.

If we are grieving for someone who has left us, either by death or by their choice, we can't help but remember them and our shared past. It's right that we do so. Our memories will be vivid, the sadness and pain will be sharp and poignant, anger and hurt may be savage and wild.

On the road of recovery we are not asked to deny our thoughts and feelings or try to block our memories. We cannot undo the effects of past experiences but we are invited to begin to change our relationship with them, to allow them to take their places in the story of our lives, integrated into our being, accepted and not fought off.

We are encouraged to look around us and notice the new things that God is doing in our lives. The very fact that we are able to explore new possibilities and are beginning to hope that our future will be brighter than our past is perhaps one of those new things.

Earlier we thought about how we need the help of an experienced professional therapist to explore past experiences that may have caused us physical, mental, emotional or sexual harm.

I prefer to use the word 'harm' rather than 'abuse'. Of course, there are people who have been deliberately and terribly abused in many different ways and I most certainly would not for one minute want to minimize their experiences of being abused. But sometimes children are harmed not by any intention or fault of their families but by a lack of maturity, understanding and self-knowledge, which complicates and damages all relationships between members of the family, including those with a child or children.

The harm done to a child's emotional development can be profound and debilitating as he or she grows into adulthood. If so much harm has been done to a child that it's still affecting her life and relationships when she is 'grown up' it will need very careful and gentle therapeutic support and guidance to help the adult reach an understanding of what's happened.

Once again, we are not called to block memories or deny the pain and harm done to us. Instead we are again invited to change our relationship with those harmful experiences and to allow them, over time, to integrate themselves into our lives and being so that they no longer hold us captive.

This therapeutic process of untangling ourselves from our past might well feel like a long journey through a barren and dry wilderness, but God promises us that he is doing a new thing in our lives and that there will be streams of water – life-giving and purifying water to refresh and revive us.

If we are remembering the former things and considering the things of old in a healthy way in order to heal our wounds, we will also be able to walk with our faces turned to the road ahead. The past will always be there in the eternal now and we will rejoin it, reconciled with our present and our future, and all of them redeemed by the God who makes all things new.

AN UNEXPECTED
INTERLUDE

Journal entry: Thursday 25 April 2013

It's been quite a while since I wrote any new material for the book. I've been thinking about it, of course, and jotting down ideas but actually writing real sentences and paragraphs has been difficult.

I've had another big dip which started before Christmas and I was afraid that I was entering into another prolonged episode of depression which would prevent me completing this work. My inner demons were telling me my writing's no good and that I'm stupid to believe the book would be published and so on.

But I'm determined to use this dip in a constructive way, to bring something positive out of what has been a very unpleasant experience. I'm going to reflect on the last three or four months and blend in anything new I've discovered with the lessons I've already learnt about recovering from and managing depression. And the first of these lessons is to do with the fear we might experience when we sense depression may be building up again inside us.

Fear not

I went to Morning Prayer on Tuesday, St George's Day, and was struck again by how often and how firmly God bids us not to be afraid and promises to be with us in all his power and glory wherever we are. Woven into the service were these words:

- 'As I was with Moses, so I will be with you; I will not fail you or forsake you' (Josh. 1.5b).
- 'I hereby command you: Be strong and courageous; do not be frightened or dismayed, for the LORD your God is with you wherever you go' (Josh. 1.9).
- 'The Lord looses those that are bound . . . The Lord lifts up those who are bowed down' (Ps. 146.7a, 8a, *CWDP*, p. 870).
- 'Finally, be strong in the Lord and in the strength of his power' (Eph. 6.10).

And those words reminded me of these:

- 'Do not fear, for I have redeemed you. I have called you by name, you are mine' (Isa. 43.1b).

I came home feeling reasonably certain that I had heard a pretty clear message from God to me during the last half an hour! Fear not!

Fear is such a powerful emotion, such a destructive force and so difficult to fight off. Fear is like a bully. It knows our weaknesses, it plays on our vulnerability and it tries to convince us that the lies it tells us are the truth.

Towards the end of last year and until two or three weeks ago I felt as if I was on a slippery slope down into deep depression again. Fear tried to tell me that I would be overwhelmed. It tried to tell me I would be as ill as I was 13 years ago but this time there would be no way out and I would finally be defeated.

This very recent encounter with fear led me to hunt down these words of Franklin D. Roosevelt from his first inaugural address in 1933: '. . . let me assert my firm belief, that the only thing we have to fear is fear itself – nameless, unreasoning, unjustified terror . . .'

I can see now that if I am afraid of experiencing another major episode of depression I am going to be too weak and vulnerable to protect myself from it. I need to be convinced that depression cannot and will not completely overwhelm me. But it's not easy to find and keep hold of such a conviction when the going gets tough. We must never underestimate the inner struggle that goes on when we are reaching out for the courage to stand up to this bully called fear.

Why does the story of Joseph come into my mind? While Joseph was in prison in Egypt Pharaoh, the king, had a dream about seven 'ugly and thin cows' eating up seven 'sleek and fat cows'. Joseph's interpretation of this dream was that Egypt would experience seven years of 'great plenty' followed by seven years of famine during which 'all the plenty will be forgotten'. Joseph's advice to Pharaoh was that the people of Egypt should use the years of plenty to put aside enough food to see them through the seven-year famine (Gen. 41.1–36).

I think my advice to myself is to use the 'times of plenty', when I am well and feeling strong, to explore and deepen my spiritual life and my relationship with God. In those times also I need to grow in knowledge and understanding of my own thoughts and emotions. By doing these things I hope that whenever depression does loom on the horizon I will have the inner resources I need to keep fear at bay.

I think that the next sections of the book are going to be about using our spiritual and mental 'times of plenty', firstly to try to avoid a time of depression altogether, secondly to learn to recognize and deal with the warning signs to which we may be particularly vulnerable, and thirdly to put in place an action plan or strategy for when depression does start getting a real hold on us.

Journal entry: Wednesday 1 May 2013

Over the last few weeks there has been an outbreak of measles in Wales which has reached epidemic proportions. Thousands of children who have not already been immunized against the disease are being vaccinated to protect them from what is a very nasty illness.

And I'm thinking, wouldn't it be great if depression was an illness like measles, chicken pox or mumps – very nasty but preventable, or only catchable once because the person then has natural immunity.

But depression just isn't like that. I think of it more like a condition with which I live, constantly aware that it's in the background all the time. Sometimes it can flare up and interfere with my everyday life to varying degrees, then it'll fade away again and I can get back to whatever 'normal' is for me at the time.

I've never known anything different, but of course many people suffer depression for the first time in their adult life. Some may make a full recovery but others (and I suspect it's the majority) are left with a sense of it lurking in the shadows, and they are vulnerable to experiencing another episode – they are not immune to it. And it can be very difficult to accept that this is the case. We may need to keep praying:

> God, give us grace to accept with serenity
> the things that cannot be changed,
> courage to change the things that should be changed,
> and the wisdom to distinguish the one from the other.[3]

I know only too well that serenity is not one of my strong points, and neither are patience and tolerance (of myself or others). But with

God's help I'm working on these and on my patterns of thinking and emotional reactions to situations which are unhelpful or even harmful to me and probably, therefore, to others as well.

Sometimes I reflect on Jesus saying that we must take up our cross and follow him, and wonder whether taking up our cross might mean summoning the courage to accept in our lives something that is a painful burden (e.g. depression) and learning how to be a disciple while carrying that burden which in this world cannot be lifted from us completely.

What I have learnt is that railing against the illness and the unfairness of it all, asking, 'Why me?' and demanding an immediate and complete recovery, while totally understandable, in the end leads nowhere and only causes more misery. At some point we have to 'face facts', 'take up our cross', accept ourselves as we are, complete with a condition called depression, and set off on the steep and rugged pathway of resurrection and new life.

Once we do that, and we may need to repeat this cycle of protesting and accepting many times, we can begin to live in the present, as it is, and learn as we walk what helps and what doesn't help us on our way.

> Father, hear the prayer we offer:
> not for ease that prayer shall be,
> but for strength that we may ever
> live our lives courageously.
>
> Not for ever in green pastures
> do we ask our way to be;
> but the steep and rugged pathway
> may we tread rejoicingly.
>
> Not for ever by still waters
> would we idly rest and stay;
> but would smite the living fountains
> from the rocks along our way.
>
> Be our strength in hours of weakness,
> in our wanderings be our guide;
> through endeavour, failure, danger,
> Father, be thou at our side.[4]

This prayerful hymn is very special to me. Try reading it through slowly and reflect on the images it suggests of God being right beside us no matter how rough things get, and how he makes it possible for us to 'tread rejoicingly'.

Part 3

BODY, MIND AND SPIRIT

7

Body, mind and spirit working together

————•◆•————

A young and relatively inexperienced tennis player faces a match against one of the top seeds who is expected to win the championship. At first our young player (let's call him Tom) gives it his all: he has nothing to lose, since no one expects him to win, and a lot to gain in terms of experience and the possibility of winning a few games. Quite unexpectedly and early in the match Tom finds himself at set point against his opponent, and suddenly his mind leaps ahead: 'What if I actually win this point, this set, this match . . . it would be sensational . . . and the next match.' Before his opponent serves, Tom sees himself in his mind's eye receiving the champion's cup. Distracted and in overdrive, his mind loses its focus and concentration; on playing this point, his return shot is wild and it's 'deuce' again.

As quickly as it leapt too far ahead in great excitement, Tom's mind now plunges down with negative thoughts and, what's worse, self-loathing. These thoughts and attitudes in turn affect his play so that in the rest of the match he only wins a handful of points and no games.

Tom has no physical energy to keep his play at the level he began with and it shows in his demeanour. His feet drag, his shoulders slouch and a strained muscle hurts more than it did before. He just wants the match to be over!

We may have seen similar reactions in various sporting events and in everyday life.

We are complex creatures with many facets to our ways of being. We have bodies, minds and spirits that interact with each other, affecting our physical health, our sense of well-being and thought processes, our emotions and the life of our innermost being, our souls.

When we're recovering from depression it's good to have a developing awareness of how we feel in body, mind and spirit and how each is affecting the others. For example:

- Clinical depression may be partially caused by a hormonal imbalance, which can be treated so that depression is lifted.
- Stress and anxiety may be behind mouth ulcers and stomach upsets.
- Chronic pain over a long period of time may be physically exhausting and lead to the development of clinical depression.
- Medication for depression may have physical side effects, and other medication (such as antibiotics) may affect our state of mind.

If this sounds negative, let's remember that it works the other way as well. Improved physical health, the effective treatment of pain or recovery from an infection will help our state of mind and raise our spirits. We may feel more motivated to look after ourselves better, to work towards better physical fitness and to socialize more with other people.

We thought earlier about recovery being like the tiny mustard seed that Jesus talks about (Matt. 13.31–32), which over time can reach our whole being with its healing power. Our task is to try to provide the best environment and care we can to allow that seed of recovery to grow. We need to be gentle and forgiving with ourselves, remembering that depression can wound us in ways that prevent us from challenging its power. It's a particularly nasty cruelty that depression can:

- sap our physical and mental energy;
- distort our thinking processes;
- cloud our judgements and decision-making abilities;
- rob us of a sense of humour;
- tell us we don't deserve to recover;
- give us a sense of isolation from other people and from God.

In other words, depression sabotages all the aspects of ourselves we most need in order to recover, and then it mocks us for even trying to get free of it.

But have you ever seen a dandelion that has pushed its way through a recently resurfaced driveway or footpath? Against all the odds, it's struggled in the dark and through a great weight of tarmac to reach the daylight and raise its head to the sun. It's staggering to think of that process and it says a lot about the determination and innate energy found in the natural world which refuses to be defeated while it can still grow.

I believe that we all have within us that kind of God-given innate energy, which is always working for our health and well-being in body, mind and spirit, sometimes in spite of our own efforts! I think this is what the Quakers call 'that of God within us', and we can trust it. The life that enables a dandelion to grow through tarmac will surely enable us to journey through the valley of shadows to a place where we can feel the sun on our faces once again.

In the next three chapters I'd like us to think about some aspects of our recovery in body, mind and spirit using verses from Psalm 139 as a framework for our reflections.

8

Caring for our bodies

———•◦•———

O Lord, you have searched me out and known me;
you know my sitting down and my rising up; . . .

You mark out my journeys and my resting place
and are acquainted with all my ways. . . .

You encompass me behind and before
and lay your hand upon me.

(Psalm 139.1a, 2, 4, *CWDP*, p. 861)

We belong to a God who has promised to be with us always. He is not
a God who stays at his desk at head office and monitors us all with
cameras and satnav systems. He doesn't communicate with us using
mobile phones, Facebook and Twitter (although he might do so from
time to time!). God is right there beside us where he can touch us.
He's within us and speaks in the silence of our hearts. He cares about
our physical state of health and the way we treat our bodies.

As we noted in the last chapter, our minds and spirits are also
affected by our physical state. So for many reasons it's important that
we pay attention to our health after a time of depression when we
may have neglected the task of taking care of our physical selves.

For example, we may not have been eating healthily, perhaps because
we just had no appetite and couldn't enjoy food or because we didn't
have the energy or motivation to cook or shop. Or we might have gone
to the other extreme (I did!) and eaten too much of all the wrong things:
chocolate, biscuits, cake and anything sweet. I was 'comfort eating' but
at the same time hating myself for putting on weight and still needing
to eat – another example of our physical state affecting our minds.

Because our energy levels were low we probably found that we were
often exhausted, worn out after the least exertion and quite unable to
contemplate even a walk round the block.

It's fair to say that depression is generally bad for your health. A more healthy diet and taking some regular exercise will almost certainly improve things over time. But do take it gently and don't be hard on yourself or push yourself to do more than you're ready for. Our bodies need care and nurturing, not bullying and overworking. Which leads me on to these verses from Psalm 139:

> For you yourself created my inmost parts;
> you knit me together in my mother's womb.
>
> I thank you, for I am fearfully and wonderfully made;
> marvellous are your works, my soul knows well.
>
> My frame was not hidden from you,
> when I was made in secret
>   and woven in the depths of the earth.
>
> Your eyes beheld my form, as yet unfinished;
> already in your book were all my members written,
>
> As day by day they were fashioned
> when as yet there was none of them.
>   (Psalm 139.12–16, *CWDP*, p. 861)

These verses give us an extraordinary picture of a God whose intimate knowledge of us reaches back to our formation in our mother's womb. There has never been a time when God has not known us as living, physical beings. God knew us long before we had any self-awareness at all and still knows us better and more deeply than we can know ourselves.

For me these verses speak of a loving and caring God. There is something very tender and gentle in the pictures of God weaving us in the secret depths of the earth and watching over us as our bodies develop in the womb.

So how sad it is when someone neglects to care for his body or even actively seeks to harm it. This is not uncommon, however, among people with depression. It happens either because of the illness itself or because of the 'hidden things' that lie behind it (see pp. 49ff.).

Depression caused Jack to have very low self-esteem and sometimes a distorted view of his own body, which he could only see as ugly and fat. He blamed himself, thus making worse the disgust and anger he felt for himself. Rather than being compassionate towards himself and nurturing his body into better health, Jack's inner pain and anger was directed back at himself in 'punishing' self-harming behaviour.

Sally reacted with this sort of angry self-hatred when she was suffering an episode of clinical depression. Her already low self-esteem took a further hammering every time she looked in the mirror or weighed herself. Her reaction was sometimes to sink into despair and feel miserable about herself and her future. Sometimes, though, she would react by hitting or punching her own body, scratching at her skin until it bled or deliberately making herself sick after her next meal.

These reactions might have been symptoms of depression which lifted with the illness as medication became effective. But there were further layers of 'stuff' underneath these symptoms which explained more about Sally's self-punishing behaviour. She had recently ended a relationship with a man who had been physically (including sexually) abusive towards her. She had had several relationships in the past where this had happened and she had come to believe at some level that she deserved such treatment. She also had memories, albeit hazy ones, of feeling threatened as a child and distressed when being bathed by someone. She had never discussed these shadows of memories and feelings with anyone until she was referred by her GP to a psychologist. Talking through all this enabled Sally, after some considerable time, to let her past rest in comparative peace and to start building a new relationship with herself in which she looked after her body, accepted herself as she was and expected others also to treat her with respect.

For Sally her physical and mental senses of well-being were inextricably linked; while both were so fragile she was very vulnerable to depression, which in turn caused her to harm herself further, thus perpetuating the downward spiral into darkness.

Our bodies, as well as our minds, can hold memories of pain and abuse. Our muscles can store stress, tension and anxiety, and sometimes treatment of such physical problems (by an osteopath, for example, or a deep massage) can release strong emotions and bring to the surface memories that had been hidden from us.

So it is important that we pay attention to what our bodies are telling us they need and that we respond with compassion to those needs.

Let's now go on to reflect on how we care for our minds.

9

Caring for our minds

———◆•◆•◆———

O Lord, you have searched me out and known me;
. . . you discern my thoughts from afar. . . .

For there is not a word on my tongue,
but you, O Lord, know it altogether. . . .

Such knowledge is too wonderful for me,
so high that I cannot attain it. . . .

Search me out, O God, and know my heart;
try me and examine my thoughts.

See if there is any way of wickedness in me
and lead me in the way everlasting.
(Psalm 139.1, 3, 5, 23, 24, *CWDP*, pp. 861–2)

'The hidden things'

I'm sure I'm not the only one who finds it scary that our God sees
through to our innermost thoughts, desires and secrets. Actually for
me it's sometimes been almost unbearable to imagine being that well
known. I have feared judgement, ridicule, shaming and punishment,
and that's just about the thoughts, desires and secrets of which I'm
aware. What about those I don't know about, the hidden things that
I haven't yet been able to face up to?

Perhaps we all have such fears. Perhaps for some it really is unbearable and they spend their lives running from themselves and God,
never able to be still and know that God is love.

Trusting in a God who is full of compassion, long-suffering and
very merciful is the only way I know of being able to approach him
with anything like an open heart and mind. But trusting isn't always
that easy.

I think it can take an enormous amount of courage to be completely open and honest with God, especially if someone else witnesses your honesty by listening as you speak of things you've kept locked up in your mind, maybe for many years. Somehow it doesn't help to be told or to think that God knows those things anyway so we might as well say it out loud. There's something significant about actually acknowledging the thoughts and speaking the words; it crosses a line that cannot be uncrossed.

The 'hidden things' in hearts and minds that might lie behind depression can take many forms.

- Peter was ashamed of the distinctly unloving feelings he had towards his brother. He was also deeply resentful towards other people who he felt were undeservedly better off than him, for example in their position at work, the house and car they could afford or the holidays they enjoyed.
- Jane was afraid of the violence of her own anger, which could erupt at any time for no readily apparent reason.
- James felt a profound sadness and grief when he heard particularly emotive music on radio or television. He was too embarrassed to talk about what he saw as a major weakness in him which he couldn't understand.
- Sandra just couldn't feel any sort of love for God or gratitude for his love for her, which she didn't really believe in anyway. She was quite unable to trust in a loving heavenly Father or Mother when her own parents had been very unpredictable and highly critical.

The 'hidden things' may not be 'big shocking secrets' that would make headline news. They're often thoughts and feelings that we all experience, but for some reason they have not been integrated healthily into our consciousness and our view of ourselves. Instead they stay locked up, sometimes festering or exploding to the surface in certain circumstances.

Some people, though, have experienced a major trauma in the past, perhaps during their childhood or more recently in their adult life. In the last chapter we met Sally, who had been profoundly damaged by the abuse she suffered in her childhood and, partly as a consequence of that abuse, in her adult relationships with men. Sally's recovery did indeed follow a painfully long and winding road. With the skilled support of a psychologist she talked about her experiences and how they affected her thinking and her emotions. She reached some degree of understanding as to why these things happened and learned how to take care of herself to prevent similar things happening again. All this took a long time and in the process Sally had to dismantle her old ways of coping, the defensive barriers she had unconsciously put up between her and other people, and her damaging view of herself as unlovable and outside the reach of God's love and healing.

For a while it seemed to Sally that things were getting far more difficult and distressing, but there was no way back. That little seed of recovery had really taken root in her heart and, sensing warmth and light not far away, was determined to break through the cold darkness. Sally could only keep going forward with slowly growing faith and hope.

Therapeutic support

Caring for our minds as we recover from depression can be a delicate task beset with dangers and risk of further harm. I want to sound a note of caution here both for those who are in the early stages of recovery and for those who love and care for such a person or who offer pastoral care as a member of the clergy or other minister.

It can be quite easy with sympathetic, or better still empathic, listening and without severe time restraints to encourage someone to open up and tell you things in confidence that she has never been able to talk about before. Initially this may feel good and right for both of you, and indeed often may be just what was needed to enable someone to move forward in their lives.

But our minds are hugely complicated and sensitive. Some very powerful and painful emotions and memories may be stirred up in an already distressed person. Her emotions may then find an outward expression that leaves her exhausted, very vulnerable and in urgent need of professional therapeutic support.

To the pastoral minister I want to say, 'Be careful'. It's not just that unprofessional intervention may not help but that it may actually cause further harm to an already hurting mind. Be careful, too, about your own well-being. When the person you want to help starts talking to you about deeply embedded difficulties in her life, you run the risk of being overwhelmed by her strong emotions and in need of support yourself. Psychotherapists or counsellors are trained to manage both their own responses to what their clients tell them and the relationships that develop with those clients. They receive supervision and have firm boundaries around their contact with their clients in terms of time, place and length of sessions. As a pastoral minister, ordained or lay, you may find it extremely difficult, if not impossible, to put in place such restrictions, but it is important that you are aware of the potential risks both to yourself and to the other person that are inherent in engaging deeply in someone's pain and neediness.

To the person in need of professional and therapeutic support I would also say, 'Be careful'. If you have deep-rooted and historical issues to deal with, please try to find a trained psychotherapist or counsellor who can give support with safe and structured boundaries and codes of behaviour for your relationship with him or her. I believe we all have to take personal responsibility for the sort of care we seek for our minds. It may be wise to err on the side of caution if you do need to begin talking about very painful experiences, thoughts and feelings that lie behind your depression.

I have had discussions with several people about whether or not a Christian should seek out a Christian psychotherapist or counsellor. Based on my own experience, my view is that the important thing is to find the right person to work with you and not worry about his or her faith. Over the years I have worked with several therapists and have found that they have all been respectful of my faith, whatever their own beliefs have been. I know others would disagree with me and say that it's essential to find a Christian counsellor. This is another area where we each have to make our own decisions as best we can, with much thought and prayer and understanding, and it may take a while to find the right person for us. If we're well clear of our 'A&E' stage of recovery we may feel more able to take our time over this and more willing to trust our own judgement and decision-making skills.

Medication

A diagnosis of clinical depression by a doctor will almost certainly bring with it a prescription for some kind of antidepressant – and there are many different kinds to choose from. They vary a great deal depending on how they work, what particular symptoms of depression they may be focused on (such as high anxiety) and the severity of the illness.

Each of us will have our own experience of taking antidepressants and I don't think there can be any hard and fast rules about it. We need to be guided by our GP or psychiatrist who will make a decision about the type of antidepressant to be prescribed and the dosage to be taken. He or she will then monitor the symptoms of depression and any side effects the drug of choice has (and almost all do have side effects).

My own experience has been of trying various types of medication, with varying degrees of success, until during my last major episode I was prescribed one that worked really well. I've tried cutting down the dose, and then stopping completely, but each time I've begun to slide down again and so have resumed taking the medication before things got worse. I now take the view that antidepressants put right some sort of chemical imbalance in my brain and I will always need to take them. They have side effects, but these don't bother me particularly and I can modify my own dosage within certain parameters.

These are some things I've learnt and situations I've come across to do with medication.

- People who are very surprised if I tell them I take antidepressants, because, they say, I don't seem to be depressed. I explain that that's because the antidepressants are working!
- Psychiatrists who say antidepressants are in fact just placebos and don't actually do anything. I really can't get my head round that one.
- People who call antidepressants 'happy pills' and who totally misunderstand the nature of the medication. For some reason I find this reaction very hard to deal with. To me it comes across as disparaging but I try to keep calm and explain the truth about what their purpose is and how they work.
- People who refuse medication because they prefer to try complementary or alternative methods of treatment. I have very little experience in these areas, although I did consult a homoeopathic practitioner for a while and found that helpful up to a point. The practitioner I saw was happy to treat me while I was taking antidepressants (I told him which ones I had been prescribed) and that may be an option for anyone who wants to try both approaches.
- People who stop taking antidepressants as soon as they begin to feel better. One psychiatrist told me that actually a person should go on taking them for 18 months after feeling well. The process

of recovery from depression is often slow and brings with it major changes in lifestyle. We need to allow time for that to happen and sometimes it's only when we do feel better that we can tackle the 'hidden things' that have been troubling us. We need stability of mind to do that, and withdrawing medication can easily upset the balance we've so recently found and send us back down into the dark.

I think in general I would say that:

- Antidepressants can and do help a lot of people in their recovery from depression.
- There is no shame in needing medication to treat what is a clinical illness any more than there is in people with diabetes needing insulin.
- For most people, antidepressants on their own probably won't cure depression. However, they can ease its symptoms so that it's possible to work on lifestyles and issues that have contributed to the development of depression in the first place.
- Side effects may be inconvenient, unpleasant and unwanted, but frankly I'd put up with most side effects if it meant I wasn't depressed any more.
- By the time you are travelling along the road of recovery with the first crisis stage behind you, you will probably have found the best antidepressant for you and will be able to monitor its effectiveness in keeping you free of some of the worse symptoms of depression.

I said earlier that caring for our mind can be a delicate task. There is usually a balance to be found between the treating of the medical mental illness of depression and identifying and bringing healing for any psychological difficulties that may be contributing to the illness. I doubt if we can ever measure those two 'ingredients' of depression and I don't think there's any need to do so. The important task for us is, with the help of doctors and appropriate therapists, to find some stability and peace for our troubled minds. It can be done with time and that work, I believe, continues for the rest of our lives, as it does for everyone. I also believe that, whether or not we have experienced the darkness of depression, the Holy Spirit within us is always working to draw us deeper and deeper into God's eternal light and life.

10

Caring for our spirits

———•◦•———

Where can I go then from your spirit?
Or where can I flee from your presence?

If I climb up to heaven, you are there;
if I make the grave my bed, you are there also.

If I take the wings of the morning
and dwell in the uttermost parts of the sea,

Even there your hand shall lead me,
your right hand hold me fast.
(Psalm 139.6–9, *CWDP*, p. 861)

During the last few years of her life my mother suffered from dementia which, as it steadily got worse, took her away from us until it seemed as if there was nothing left of the real 'her'. I'm sure others in similar situations ask the same sort of questions I did about the cruelty of dementia and why it was happening to this particular person.

Unable to grieve properly because physically she was still alive, but at the same time unable to relate to her as the person she was, my big questions were: 'Where is she now? Where has her spirit gone?' A friend responded to my question by saying, 'I don't know, but God is with her.' That statement of faith was a huge comfort to me. The God who has promised men and women down the ages that 'I will be with you' will keep that promise for ever, and no one can be separated from the loving presence of God whose right hand holds us fast.

During an episode of depression we may feel that our 'real' selves have been buried and crushed under the heavy weights we carry. Others may also have difficulty seeing our 'real' selves. They say things like, 'You're not yourself' or 'This is so unlike you'. I know I've felt like that about people close to me who have been going through times of depression.

When we feel so detached from our 'real' selves or so devastatingly alone that it seems that God has forsaken us we may not be able to hold on to God's promise always to be with us. We may need to rely on others believing that for us and trying to reassure us that in the end 'all shall be well'.

One of the most insensitive and unhelpful things that can be said to someone who is depressed is surely, 'Pull yourself together!' Ironically, though, I once found myself visualizing my experience of recovery in which 'pulling myself together' was in a sense what I was doing.

I imagined my soul, my deepest being, as a large mirror which got smashed. All the pieces were lying around in lots of different sizes and shapes, with a broken but surviving little 'me' at the centre. I imagined all those pieces slowly, very slowly, drawing back together again and gently uniting as one piece, with a not so little 'me' still at the centre. It was a bit like showing a film of a mirror being smashed and then watching that film backwards at a very slow speed. Of course, in that film the mirror would end up perfect, as it was before being broken, whereas when we have 'pulled ourselves together', reintegrated our broken selves, we will perhaps have visible crack lines and a new fragility but we won't be in pieces any more and we will be able to live our lives more effectively and more richly.

So how do we care for our spirits as we go through the illness and on to recovery and integration? What helps me are the sort of things that I can hang on to as being 'real' and 'true'. For example:

- During a midweek service of Holy Communion my birth certificate was on the altar as a symbol of my existence. At a time when I felt as if I had no right to be alive and was full of hatred and disgust for myself, this experience gave me an assurance of God's love and blessing. It told me that I am meant to be alive and that I am loved by God and also by the people supporting me. And there were witnesses who could remind me of this whenever doubts returned.
- More than once I have received anointing with oil and prayer for healing with laying on of hands.
- Thirteen years on I still carry with me a postcard someone gave me when I was finding it hard to believe that anyone would want me around, especially those I regularly met with at Morning Prayer. The card depicts 'The dragon cast into the jaws of hell' from the

Lambeth Apocalypse. The message reads: *Katharine – banish the dragon of doubt! We are on your side – so don't be shy, don't hide away and don't be afraid to come out and pray!!!*

Quite often in various services, on quiet days or in any place of prayer we are invited to do something practical and symbolic: write a prayer card, light a candle, place a stone in water and so on. Usually, though, when I do this I cannot make the symbolic actions *feel* meaningful or healing. In my head I may understand their meaning and hope that somehow they will make a difference, but my heart and my spirit are often left untouched and nothing seems to change. Perhaps you've experienced this too. But a prayer through some symbolic action *is* a prayer (and one that we can remember offering), and God is always ready to listen, to receive and to respond to such prayer. We may not be aware at the time of any change, but we have, once again, been nurturing that seed of recovery and growth by opening up a little more to God's healing spirit.

When we are caring for our spirits and looking for ways to let God into our lives I think it's important to be very honest with ourselves, although that's not always easy. It's not easy either to be totally honest with God. It can be very painful to stand spiritually naked before God knowing that he sees us as we really are in all our messy confusion with doubts and fears that hold us back.

But while God sees us as we are he also loves us and wishes us only what is healing and beautiful. I love these words from Isaiah, which help me to trust in God's gentleness and loving-kindness:

Here is my servant, whom I uphold, my chosen, in whom my soul delights; . . . a bruised reed he will not break, and a dimly burning wick he will not quench.   (Isa. 42.1a, 3a)

11

Some ideas for day-to-day living

In this chapter I'm going to share with you a few ideas about our day-to-day care of our bodies, minds and spirits. I hope you may find some of these suggestions helpful, perhaps opening up one or two previously unnoticed paths along the road or encouraging you to explore new ways of caring for yourself in body, mind and spirit.

They are not 'rules' and not all of them will be of use to everyone. It's a case of 'take your pick' and do with them as you wish!

Spiritual food

If our faith is to grow and deepen we do need to pay attention to our spiritual life, and if we are in any kind of ministry or hold an office within the church that requires our attention on Sundays as well as during the week we may need to seek spiritual food in other places and at other times.

I continue to attend Morning Prayer each weekday, and those of us who are there share in leading, reading and praying. Because it's very informal we also quite often share thoughts and ideas about the readings or other insights we've had. You might think about whether this is a possibility for you.

We may want to have a set time each day for reading Scripture, reflecting and praying, or we may set aside a longer time on two or three days of the week. Or we may have regular walks during which we find ourselves talking with God, which is what praying really is. God is happy to talk with us at any time and anywhere; he doesn't need us to adopt a particular posture at a particular place at home or in church.

At the end of this book I suggest various books that I've found helpful in this process of recovery, but I'd like to mention here one in particular: *Spirituality for Everyday Living: An adaptation of the Rule of St Benedict* by Brian C. Taylor.[5] It's a slim book (70 pages), easy to read and full of ideas and suggestions about building up our spiritual life without insisting on rigid rules and schedules.

The important thing in our spiritual lives is to make sure we don't make demands of ourselves that become a huge burden weighing us down – depressing us. That's not what God wants of us. There's a lovely piece in Eugene H. Peterson's *The Message* from Matthew 11 when Jesus says:

> Are you tired? Worn out? Burned out on religion? Come to me. Get away with me and you'll recover your life. I'll show you how to take a real rest. Walk with me and work with me – watch how I do it. Learn the unforced rhythms of grace. I won't lay anything heavy or ill-fitting on you. Keep company with me and you'll learn to live freely and lightly.

How does that sound to you?

Keeping a journal

Through the years writing a journal has been therapeutic for me and might perhaps help you in your journey. I've been able to express in writing thoughts and feelings that would otherwise have no outlet. Getting them all down on paper and offering them to God as prayer has almost always moved things on a little for me and cleared a bit of space for my next step.

There are other benefits. When I read back what I've written, after enough time has passed, I can often see how prayers have been answered although not necessarily as I wanted or expected. I can see how far I've come without realizing it and I can pick out recurrent themes and patterns of thought processes and behaviour that are either unhelpful or, on the other hand, positive and affirming.

Keep it simple; it doesn't have to be a great work of literature – just a few notes to remind yourself of things that are happening, how you're feeling and anything that's important to you on that particular day.

Medical check-ups

It's possible that during an episode of depression you have not felt able to commit to things like dental appointments or go to your optician for a regular eye test. If that's the case it might be an idea to get these sorts of things up to date. Some medication can affect things like your teeth and your eyesight and it may help any practitioner you see to know what your doctor has prescribed, so that this can be taken into account.

You may also still be experiencing symptoms that were either assumed to be symptoms of depression or were hidden by your general physical and mental malaise while deeply depressed. If you are, it might be good to get those checked out by your GP (I'm thinking here of things like dizzy spells, frequent headaches and, for women, premenstrual tension).

If you need to pay attention to your diet and how much exercise you take now that you're out of the early days of recovery, your GP can give you support and advice for that as well. It'll be important not to do too much too soon but to build up your strength and change your eating habits at a pace you can cope with.

Tiredness can kill – take a break!

We see road signs giving us this message about driving, and I've spoken to motorists who say that tiredness can creep up on you: it's possible to be overcome by sleepiness with little or no warning. Experience tells me that stress and depression can also catch us out with little warning when we're overtired. Being tired seems to be a very common state of being for a lot of people, but we need to watch out for it in ourselves if we want to keep from drifting into dark places of the mind.

There are obvious ways of avoiding overtiredness: going to bed at a time that allows us enough sleep; planning space in our diary following a particularly busy day or week; not taking on too many 'extras' on top of our normal commitments. But it's possible we may need to take a step back and assess how realistic we're being about what we can and can't do. I know it's difficult when there are a lot of things 'booked in' and we want to do all of them, but sometimes we do have to sacrifice something in order to protect ourselves from being overtired and therefore vulnerable.

Be good to yourself – you're worth it!

Adrian goes once a month to have an aromatherapy massage of his back, neck and shoulders. He derives great benefit from this. When he's working he's mostly sitting at his desk or driving long distances so this sort of massage helps his muscles to relax. It also helps with his stress levels, which are often quite high, and the tension this builds up in those same muscles.

Soaking in a hot bath with favourite oils, having a foot massage, some sort of treatment for our hair, making time to listen to music or a radio programme we particularly enjoy: paying this sort of attention to our minds and bodies can bring healing into our day-to-day lives. We are giving ourselves the message that, yes, 'we're worth it', and it's good to be kind and gentle with ourselves.

A balancing exercise

I work at home and spend a lot of time sitting at my desk writing or in front of the computer. The work I do can be pretty intense: commissioned pieces, material for my website, sermons or prayers for services, research and planning for study groups and so on.

When I was down in the recent dip I've spoken about I realized that I needed to focus on my need for exercise and to do something that was fun and with other people. As I write I'm hoping to start voluntary work at a local riding centre for the disabled which 'ticks all the boxes' as well as appealing to my love of horses. I've done this work before and know how therapeutic it can be for the riders to have the experience of horse riding and I'm really looking forward to being involved again.

Maybe you could do with some sort of variation in your lifestyle to make it feel more balanced and rounded. It's worth thinking about, especially if you are in a caring profession and giving of yourself to others in your working day. Take some time to do something for yourself and enjoy the nourishment that can give to your body, mind and spirit.

Prayer for healing of body, mind and spirit

I'd like to end this section with a prayer particularly for those who have been physically, sexually, emotionally or spiritually harmed.

Heavenly Father, we thank you
for your intimate and loving knowledge of who we are
and how we are made.

In Jesus you know the damage that can be done
to our bodies, our minds and our spirits
when we are mistreated by others.
You know what it is to be humiliated, shamed and
    forsaken.
We bring to you our whole selves: body, mind and spirit.

We pray that where there is hurt you will heal us;
where we are broken you will make us whole;
where there is shame and self-loathing
you will restore dignity, self-acceptance
and a knowledge of ourselves as your beloved children;

Where there is loneliness and isolation
pour out your Holy Spirit to make known to us
your loving presence in our lives.

We thank you that we are wonderfully made
and we ask you to restore in us
unity of body, mind and spirit
within the love of our Lord Jesus Christ. Amen.

The peace of the Lord be always with you.

Part 4

ALPHA AND OMEGA

―――――・◆・―――――

> Christ yesterday and today,
> the beginning and the end,
> Alpha and Omega,
> all time belongs to him,
> and all ages;
> to him be glory and power
> through every age and for ever.
> ('The Service of Light',
> Easter Liturgy)[6]

Our starting point in this section is the story of God speaking to Moses from a burning bush (Exodus 3). God tells Moses that he has heard the cries of the people of Israel who are held in slavery in Egypt and is going to free them from that oppression. God then says to Moses, 'I will send you to Pharaoh to bring my people . . . out of Egypt' (Exod. 3.10).

Moses has various questions and protests, one of which is about what he should say to the Israelites when they ask who sent him to them. God replies, 'I AM WHO I AM'; 'you shall say to the Israelites "I AM has sent me to you"', and 'This is my name for ever, and this my title for all generations' (from Exod. 3.14–15).

The Eternal Name of God is I AM; there is no past or future, simply an eternal being outside of time.

And Jesus identifies himself with this Eternal Name. In one of his many confrontations with the religious leaders of his time Jesus says, 'Very truly, I tell you, before Abraham was, I am.' It's a shocking statement, and his Jewish listeners want to stone him for it (John 8.58).

We may not feel the same shock as these Jews did but it's still a huge concept to grasp hold of: that outside time, in the eternal, there is no past, present or future – they are all held by God in his Eternal Name.

In Chapter 3 of this book I talked about how an episode of depression can give us a different perspective on our lives, which may come to have new markers: Before, During and After the Darkness. I said that these are not separate distinct stages but they will blend together to become our present reality in which we will need to learn to live. In the next two chapters we'll be thinking more about how we may enable this process of integration to unfold in our lives.

If this seems to us a daunting prospect, let's remember that Moses also felt daunted: 'Who am I that I should go to Pharaoh, and bring the Israelites out of Egypt?' And God will say to us, as he did to Moses, 'I will be with you' (Exod. 3.11–12).

He will be with us, revealing patterns, links and pathways that will lead us to freedom from the oppression of the past and the captivity of depression.

12

Emotions of the past

Pandas and thunderstorms

Ever since I can remember, whenever there's a thunderstorm around me, in real life or on television, a picture comes into my mind of the soft black and white face of a giant panda. For a long time I had no idea why that was. I wondered if it had anything to do with the '–nder' and '–nda' sounds of the words, but that didn't seem very likely to me. It wasn't until I was in my thirties that it occurred to me to ask my family if they could think of any reason why my mind held that association. I asked my mother first. It took her less than 30 seconds to come up with the answer!

Once when I was very young (less than five years old) there was a heavy thunderstorm. It so happened that one of my favourite soft toys, a panda, had been put through the wash that morning and was out in the pouring rain pegged by his ears to the washing line. I got very distressed about this and someone went out to rescue him for me. I have no memory of this at all although I do remember the panda – he may even still be around in someone's loft!

I think it's amazing how our minds make links like that all by themselves without our conscious knowledge. Someone once said to me that there are no such things as irrational thoughts or feelings; there are only thoughts and feelings for which we have not yet uncovered the reason, which is held in our minds somewhere. My association of pandas with thunder seemed irrational yet there was a perfectly rational explanation to be found.

The known and the unknown

My association of thunder and pandas didn't carry for me any emotional element. I'm not afraid of thunder or lightning, or giant pandas come to that although I wouldn't want to get too close to one! The association came from what was obviously a very upsetting incident, of a much loved soft toy left hanging out in the rain. But my panda was rescued and no doubt I quickly cheered up and all was well.

But what if we have associations that do carry with them very strong emotions? Earlier, in Chapter 9, we met James who often felt profound sadness and grief when listening to music. The grief was very strong and went very deep, deeper than he could cope with, and he would turn the music off if he could.

We might all have had an experience of this kind when something evokes feelings of deep sadness, paralysing fear, or maybe emotions we can't put a name to.

We might know why this happens – a particular place may remind us of a sad meeting with someone we never saw again, or a certain hymn might always bring back sad or painful memories, of the funeral of a loved one or our marriage service after the death of our husband or wife.

On the other hand we might not understand why this happens. We may have no memory to explain it, just I had forgotten about my poor soggy panda. Or perhaps there was something that felt so unbearable to us at the time that our minds suppressed the memory and kept it hidden from us for our own protection.

These associations that trigger painful and distressing memories or emotions can be among the 'hidden things' that lie behind our depression. Indeed, they are literally being depressed, pushed down. That takes a lot of mental and emotional energy, leaving little to spend on our day-to-day living in the present.

Therapeutic processes

I've already suggested that we may need professional help to work through the issues raised by these powerful 'hidden things'. My own experience has taught me some lessons about this process:

- That it can be very long and drawn out with many stops and starts, ups and downs and much going round in circles. I also know it can take a lot of courage and faith in our own in-built sun-seeking dandelions.

- That it is possible to come through these experiences so that our past, although unchanged, may be seen from a new perspective and from within a new relationship with it so that it no longer has us in its grip.
- That while we are working through our mental pain and distress at a psychological level we can also bring them to God at a deeply spiritual level with the faith that it is never too late for him to heal our past.
- That there is too much specialist knowledge and training needed in both the psychological and the spiritual dimensions for one person or one group to be able to do this work with us effectively. It may be possible for our professional helpers to work as a team to support us. I'm sure that others will have had different experiences and may have been able to work with one person on all levels of their being, but it's not a situation I've known.
- That there are many things we can do to help ourselves if we can find ways of 'working through' or 'praying through' experiences and memories that are troubling us.

Bringing the emotions of the past into the 'now'

James – music and sorrow

We talked earlier about James, whom we first met in Chapter 9. Although with the support of a counsellor James tried to identify the reason for his intense grief on hearing music, he was unable to do so. He was aware, however, that he held on to that grief and thought it would be a weakness in him to 'give in' to it and weep.

Eventually he understood that although he didn't know what lay behind it, his grief was very real and needed to be expressed in a way that had not been possible until now.

Alone, but knowing that one or two people he trusted were praying for him, James lit a candle as a reminder of God's presence with him, and played a recording of music that evoked for him deep feelings of grief. He sat quietly and allowed the sadness in him to come to the surface. He wept in a way he would once have considered weak and childish. Something hard and ungiving was washed away with those tears, although he never did discover where they came from. It seemed that they just needed to be shed now because they hadn't been allowed to flow in the past. In the future that music might make

James feel sad but it will be a peaceful sadness that is no longer fighting to be acknowledged.

Jane – the clenched fist

We also met Jane in Chapter 9. She was frightened of the violence of her own anger, which could erupt at any time on a scale out of all proportion to its cause.

We all get angry about things, with other people or in certain situations: a long delay on the London Underground or being stuck behind the person in the queue at the supermarket checkout who only thinks of hunting for her purse after all her shopping has been packed and it's probably at the bottom of one of her three or four full bags! (Who's got wound up just thinking about that?)

But Jane's anger would smoulder away, fuelled by resentment and feelings of powerlessness. A person less self-controlled might have been shouting and swearing; a more aggressive person might actually have been violent towards others or taken his anger out on inanimate objects. But Jane was very self-controlled and she never actually lashed out with tongue or fist. She was more likely to end up shutting herself away and crying her eyes out, alone.

Like James, Jane never fully understood why her emotions were so strong that they almost overwhelmed her. But again, the emotions were real and needed understanding and expression. When asked by her therapist how old she felt when she was crying tears of rage she realized the experience was like a very young child having a tantrum. Immediately that brought her some understanding of how she felt. A small child lives in the 'now', and what's happening around her is all there is. If what's happening makes her angry then she's angry with her whole being and at her whole world. And she is powerless apart from her fury, which carries her away into a horrible lonely place. Expressing that level of rage is acceptable when we're aged three or four but if we're 30-something and working in an office environment it is neither appropriate nor acceptable.

As well as working on all this with a psychotherapist, Jane was discussing it with her 'soul friend' who was offering pastoral care, spiritual support and guidance. This lady wondered if Jane might also feel anger towards God: that she might believe that God had made some very upsetting things happen to her or had at least allowed them to happen rather than preventing them. Jane recognized that possibility, and then felt a huge sense of relief that that was out in the open and it was safe to talk about it.

Jane, her therapist and her soul friend met together and found ways of helping Jane to experience fully her anger and her sense of power-lessness and to express that anger safely in an atmosphere of acceptance and prayer. Jane also learned that, unlike the small child she had been, as an adult she could take responsibility for the way she acted on her emotions and was no longer powerless to change her situation.

This was a long process but it did lead to a new freedom for Jane. Of course, she still would feel anger but it would be within what we might call 'normal' levels. She was no longer afraid of the strength of her own feelings.

Sally – healing memories

Sally, whom we met in Chapter 8, was deeply troubled by distressing memories of being harmed in some way in her early childhood. Within the safety of a therapeutic relationship with a counsellor, these and more memories came to the surface of her conscious mind, along with all the emotions attached to them. Over time Sally was able to talk about these memories and feelings so that she understood why she would have felt as she did and why these past events were still affecting her so profoundly.

Sally used her artistic talents to paint abstract representations of her feelings – all her anger, hurt and fear. She then talked with a minister about the artwork and the feelings it portrayed before offering it to God, asking for healing of these emotions and the memories that carried them.

From then on, when the memories returned Sally had a sense of God being with her during those times of hurt and fear and that aware-ness brought the healing she needed, although it took months for her to reach a level of peace within herself that allowed her to live without the inner turmoil that had triggered an episode of depression.

Sandra – regaining the 'self'

Sandra was another person we met in Chapter 9. Her parents (who were regular churchgoers) had been unpredictable in their emotional responses to her and could be highly critical of things she said or did. Their behaviour wasn't intentionally abusive – it came from their own backgrounds and lack of self-awareness – but it greatly harmed Sandra's emotional development.

Sandra began seeing a counsellor who helped her to understand her feelings and thought processes and from there to develop new ways of living freed from the captivity of her past. Sandra came to understand how, quite unconsciously, she had coped as a child with her difficult relationship with her parents:

- As a child she had often felt angry about things her parents said to her and the way they judged her quite critically and unfairly. It wasn't 'safe' for her to be angry with her parents so her anger got suppressed and bottled up and became a very powerful contributing factor in Sandra's depression.
- Because her parents' reactions to her were unpredictable Sandra learned not to say or do anything spontaneously. She learned to check herself and to think about possible parental responses to whatever she might say or do, and what would prompt a positive response or at least a relatively harmless negative one.
- Over time she began giving up making that effort and slipped more and more deeply into a world of her own. Sandra's sense of powerlessness and withdrawal to avoid criticism or harsh judgement was also instrumental in causing depression.
- Sandra had lost much of her ability to make her own decisions and choices because she had feared the consequences of doing so. It had always been so important for her to work out what her parents wanted her to do that in fact she didn't really know what her own wishes and feelings were at any given time. Not surprisingly, this had added to the anger building up inside her.

Given this background we can understand why Sandra had difficulty in her relationship with a God who is described as a loving parent and in whom her parents believed. Her picture of God, which emerged during counselling, was of a critical judge who was unpredictable, unfair and demanding. Her anger with her parents spilled over into anger with God and a deep distrust of anyone who claimed to love her.

Sandra needed to learn to care for herself (in effect to be a loving parent to herself); to attend to her own needs; to be compassionate towards her weaknesses and to make decisions based on what she wanted and needed for her own healing and growth; and to trust other people, beginning with her counsellor and her spiritual guide who helped her to understand more about the true nature of God's love.

For Sandra, the process of recovery involved recognizing and under-standing her unhelpful feelings and thoughts, dismantling her ways of being based on those thoughts and feelings while also building up a new sense of self and others from which she could live a healthier and more authentic life of her own.

She also found that she needed to learn a lot about forgiveness and grieving, and we will be looking at these issues later in this book.

My way

I hope that these four stories might show how complex (and exhaust-ing!) this process of emotional and spiritual recovery can be and how much care is needed to make it safe. I hope they also show something of the need for us all to be true to our own stories, and to find or be helped to find our own ways of working at the emotional level and allowing God to work with us in our spiritual struggle.

I'm very aware that I find writing, visualization and reasoning most helpful. I'm not particularly good at expressing myself in any kind of art or craft work and I'd find it hard to work out my anger by beating cushions with a huge plastic baseball stick – I did try once and just felt silly even though I could sense what a powerful release it might be for others.

I think what I'm trying to say is that when we're seeking ways of healing and recovery each of us needs to find what's right for us, and only we can know what feels comfortable and safe. I'd like to suggest some 'golden rules':

- Be yourself, and if you're not sure who you are yet, go with what you do know and that will lead you on.
- Be as honest with yourself as you can be no matter how painful that is.
- Be as honest with others as you can be while still feeling safe in yourself. In this process you are very vulnerable, so protect your-self from anyone or anything that might undermine or hold back your recovery.
- Be as honest with God about yourself as you can be, remembering that he'll be far more understanding and compassionate towards you than you are to yourself and that he longs to set you free from your past and all that's held you captive.

13

Thinking from the past

———•◆•———

In the last chapter we thought about strong emotions which have their roots in the past and which have perhaps never been fully understood or expressed, so that they continue to cause problems for us in the present.

I'd like now to consider unhelpful patterns of thinking which we may have developed either as part of the illness of depression or as a result of early experiences, and what we learned about ourselves and others through those experiences. These are patterns of thinking that may slow down or prevent our recovery, and again it may be that we need some kind of professional help to work through them and reach a healthier understanding of ourselves and our relationships with others and the world around us.

I think that probably everyone will recognize these patterns in their own thinking: they are by no means limited to people with mental health difficulties. But sometimes these ways of thinking reveal a perception of the world around us that is outdated and needs revision if it is to stop interfering with our day-to-day living.

So let's look at just some of these patterns of thought, how they might be affecting our lives now and how we can start updating them to reflect our present reality.

It's all or nothing

As Sandra began reflecting on her patterns of thought she realized that she tended to think in clear, polarized terms of black or white, right or wrong, good or bad and so on. This kind of thinking is often present in the minds of people who are depressed but Sandra could also trace it back to her way of seeing things as a child and teenager. Her parents would make these sorts of clear judgements with few grey areas of uncertainty or indecision. They were like that about many things in life and Sandra felt that she too was judged in that way. She always seemed to be a 'good Sandra' or a 'bad Sandra'. She seldom felt loved and accepted just because she was Sandra. She learned to think about herself and others along these lines as well, but that wasn't helping her to grow and develop more mature ways of thinking.

Unfortunately, at one point in her life she had been part of a group of Christians who also tended to see things as right or wrong, good or evil, and people as being us or them, in or out. Such a rigid form of Christianity allowed little room for the confusion, doubt and distress that Sandra was experiencing in her spiritual life; it was all too messy for them, and their responses to her made Sandra feel rejected and lonely, guilty and angry. For a long time she stayed away from any kind of formal religion.

If we are thinking in this 'all or nothing' way, about our faith in particular or our life in general, it may be because we are seeking security or certainty. We perhaps find it very hard to cope with frightening uncertainty and mixed feelings. I remember once feeling very bothered about all sorts of uncertainties in my working life, my home life and in my social and church lives. I felt as if I had nothing stable to hang on to. A very wise friend said to me, 'But there is one certainty and that is that you're uncertain, so for now you just need to be able to live with that certain uncertainty.' It sounded weird at the time but it also made sense. I tried to slow down the frantic speculation going on in my head: 'What if this happens? What if that doesn't happen? Supposing I can't do this or that?' I tried instead to be still and know that God was working in all my chaos, bringing a pattern and order into it that I wouldn't be able to see until I looked back on that time from a distance of several years.

Whether our 'all or nothing' thinking is part of our illness or has its roots in earlier times, it's not a helpful way of looking at the world. It's quite shallow and superficial. It doesn't take account of the complex layers lying beneath the surface.

When we read about Jesus meeting all sorts of people we get the feeling that he senses what's going on for each one of them beyond the obvious, and he loves them no matter what those 'hidden things' might be. The stories of the Samaritan woman at the well (John 4.5–42), the woman taken in adultery (John 8.2–11) and the father whose son is possessed by an unclean spirit (Mark 9.14–27) are just three examples of Jesus meeting people at their place of pain and need, accepting them as they are and enabling them to move forward in their lives freed from their past.

Peter, another of our acquaintances from Chapter 9, tended to think in an 'all or nothing' way. In his depressed state it seemed to him that everyone around him was happy and leading perfect lives. He believed that no one could possibly feel as low and miserable as he did. And for him 'being well' would mean never feeling sadness, fear, anger or guilt.

Part of Peter's recovery was about understanding that the way he was thinking was unrealistic. Most people experience some of those feelings some of the time and he needed to relearn what would be 'normal' and realistic for him in his 'After the Darkness' time. This was quite hard for Peter, especially in the early days of recovery. It took him a while to learn the difference between the sort of 'off day' that everyone has from time to time and the sort of 'off day' that carried with it that intangible sense of heavy doom that was all too familiar to him as a symptom of depression.

For Peter there was another layer of thinking which came from his past experiences. As well as thinking that his life 'should' follow certain paths (he 'should' always be happy), Peter tended to take things very personally when they didn't go to plan: 'the universe is against me'. He would feel that the whole universe was ganging up on him when things went wrong, from the car running out of petrol to the time he didn't get the job he wanted and felt he 'should' have got.

Peter, with courageous honesty, recognized that on such occasions he felt like a toddler who is furious with all his being that he can't have what he wants and is raging against a world that has done this to him. He felt like a powerless victim in a cruel world with a tendency to be self-pitying.

New thinking

Both Sandra and Peter needed to learn to think differently about setbacks, irritations and uncertainties and about people they'd learnt to see as enemies or a threat to their way of life.

This did *not* mean that they had to deny or belittle how they were feeling, as I hope the previous chapter on emotions shows. It did mean, however, that they needed to develop new and healthier ways of dealing with these thoughts and feelings which would enable them to manage their lives more effectively.

This, of course, is far easier said than done and we must never underestimate the courage, commitment and determination Sandra and Peter needed to turn their thinking around in this way. But I remember once myself getting all het up and angry with someone who I felt sure was deliberately trying to make my life as difficult and unpleasant as possible. I can't explain what happened next. I didn't actually see anyone or hear a voice but I had a distinct sense of someone digging me in the ribs and saying, with a wink and a smile, 'Oh, come on Katharine, don't be so daft!' There was such deep love and understanding behind this that I heard it not as a rebuke but as an invitation to share a laugh at my own absurd thinking. That happened over 33 years ago but it has stayed with me and reminds me not to take myself too seriously.

When we read the Gospels we find Jesus, the Son of Man, fully human and experiencing everything that we do. He knows all our vulnerabilities, the challenges we face and the way our lives often take unexpected twists and turns. He knows that hardships, diseases, losses and failures, shocks and disappointments can happen to anyone, including him, at any time. Yet Jesus is always true to himself. He might be the victim of terrible injustice and cruelty but somehow, even on the cross, he refuses to respond with anything but love and forgiveness to those who brutalize him.

He calls us to follow him and to learn to take responsibility for ourselves so that we grow into being the people God wants us to be, our fear cast out by his perfect love and grace.

I know what you're thinking

One of the symptoms or effects of depression is that we can become extremely self-centred, tending to think that everything is about us and not in a good way. If we phone someone and they don't ring back it's because they don't want to speak to us, if we see someone in town and they don't stop for a chat they're avoiding us, if a friend doesn't comment on our new hairstyle they don't like it or think we're ugly. And so on! We find it hard to believe that there might be reasons for these things that have nothing to do with us. As we move away from the early days of depression we will probably see the funny side of this and resume more realistic thinking, accepting that we're not the centre of everyone else's world.

But what happens if this way of thinking goes back to those 'hidden things' and is not so easily shrugged off?

Let's return to Sandra's story. As we have seen, her parents were judgemental and highly critical towards people in general and towards Sandra in particular. They were sometimes very unfair in their judgement of her. They would attribute motives to her which, as she was a child, would not have been in her mind at all. They would accuse her, for example, of deliberately getting her clothes dirty, thus creating more work for her mum, or doing something she shouldn't on purpose to annoy them, wind them up or upset them. Growing up in this sort of environment affected Sandra in various ways.

- As a child she began to see herself as the sort of person her parents seemed to think she was: selfish, unkind and thoughtless. Along with such a negative self-image she also developed a generalized sense of shame about herself, which seriously undermined her self-confidence and her ability to form friendships at school.
- Because her parents thought this way about her, and because as a child it's hard or unsafe to entertain the idea that your parents are wrong, Sandra grew up believing that everyone else must see her in the same light and think in the same way about her. This led to her being very defensive in her relationships with other people, as she was expecting them to react in a negative way to anything she said or did. Unfortunately, her defensiveness often provoked from others the sort of negative response she expected and so her patterns of thinking were reinforced.
- Sandra found it very hard to hear messages that offered her a different picture of herself. She tended not to believe that she had anything to offer others in friendship or that she could do well academically or otherwise.
- Sandra also grew up adopting her parents' way of looking at the world because their way was all she knew. She tended to be critical and judgemental and to attribute to others certain feelings, motives and attitudes for which she had little or no evidence. This added to her tendency to think, 'The universe is against me', and stoked up the anger she felt within herself already.

For Sandra recovery meant recognizing her unhelpful ways of thinking, understanding how these might have developed, and learning to check her assumptions against reality.

I'd like to offer two reflections on this process and its importance in our relationships including, perhaps especially, those within our church fellowships.

First, I said a little earlier that we need courage, commitment and determination as we learn to turn unhelpful patterns of thought around. I think that's got a lot to do with the fact that we need a degree of honesty about ourselves that feels almost brutal.

Both Sandra and Peter needed to have the courage to acknowledge how critical and resentful they could be and how unfair some of their assumptions were. It's not easy being that honest, especially when you're hard on yourself and are expecting others also to judge you harshly. If we find we need professional therapeutic support we will need to build up a relationship of trust with the person providing that support, so that we feel safe when we share our thinking with him or her.

Second, within our relationships with others we can be very destructive and cause a lot of hurt and damage if we are continually assuming the worst of people before we check out the facts – the reality. Let's take a small (fictional) example.

There is a group of people within a church who enjoy getting together to watch a film at the cinema and then going for a drink or a meal afterwards. On one occasion such an outing is planned at the last minute and someone who usually goes along doesn't get to hear about it. There's nothing deliberate about this; there is no plot to exclude this person or to hurt her, it is just one of those things – perhaps everyone thought that someone else was contacting her.

The person who misses out may feel disappointed, angry or hurt – those would be understandable emotional reactions. The potential problem arises in the way the person deals with her feelings. They might be short-lived and be neutralized by a philosophical attitude that accepts what the other members of the group say and believes that there was no hostility involved. But what happens if that hurt and anger explode because the person thinks that it was deliberate – the others didn't want her there, they forgot about her because she was so unimportant to them, they were trying to push her out of the group? Such a reaction ignores the evidence that these are not unkind, thoughtless people. They have always welcomed her as an equal member of the group and are very sorry this has happened. The 'victim's' way of thinking distorts her view of these other people and causes a rift which could escalate and has the potential to spread into the wider fellowship of the church.

I hope this example may show how we can do people great injustices and cause harmful divisions within a fellowship if we fail to monitor the way we think about others and check the assumptions we make about what is going on in people's minds. If we ever find ourselves thinking badly about someone it might be worth taking a moment to ask ourselves if they really are the sort of person who would do or say such a thing or whether it's possible there's been some sort of misunderstanding.

Maybe we could make a rule for ourselves to try to think of others what we would have them think of us, and see if that helps us to move on and grow.

I have to be perfect

Imagine for a moment that a young child, perhaps your own child, grandchild, nephew or niece, has just brought you a picture he or she has made especially for you. It's on a large sheet of paper with pieces of tissue and some glitter stuck on with glue that has clearly been spread with great enthusiasm! You're not quite sure what the picture is with its bright colours and interesting shapes, but it's a gift for you from this child and naturally you're absolutely delighted with it. You accept it with joy and admiration – and never mind, you can unstick your fingers later!

We wouldn't for one minute dream of finding fault with this gift nor would we have wanted this child to be upset about something that had gone wrong with it or to have got stressed out in its creation.

But how often are we as accepting as this when it comes to our own efforts?

Perfectionism seems to me to be a common personality trait in people who suffer with depression. We don't allow ourselves to make mistakes, so when we inevitably do slip up in some way we really give ourselves a hard time. When I'm handwriting a piece of work I find it very hard to cross something out or amend what I've written. I really want to tear the page out and start all over again. This, of course, is just not realistic – it's too time-consuming and uses too many trees! I was like this at school and would get upset if I had to erase something or left a word out of a sentence. I would get swamped with the feeling that I must be useless, unable to get anything right.

I have a friend who got angry and frustrated with himself because after just a few hours of tuition he hadn't become a skilled builder of dry stone walls! Within a very short space of time he was beating himself up mentally for being hopeless at everything he tried to do. This was so far from the truth that it would have been ludicrously funny if it hadn't been so dreadfully sad.

Those of us who demand perfection of ourselves will probably never find it easy to say, 'Well, that's the best I can do today', as we finish a task or any creative activity. But let's think again about being given a picture made especially for us by a child and let's think of ourselves as children of God offering him the best we can do in our lives. If we can joyfully accept a gift from a child, however messy it is and full of mistakes, surely God will joyfully accept what we offer him and delight in our imperfect and fragile creation because we offer it in faith and love.

Maybe we need to learn to take pride and pleasure in our own imperfect work or creation and to be as gentle and loving with ourselves as God is.

The art of thinking

If you are a perfectionist the chances are that you will expect far too much of yourself when it comes to changing your ways of thinking. Do try not to do that. Our patterns of thinking, our attitudes towards others and our assumptions about what's going on in their minds have developed slowly over a long period of time. We may need only to fine-tune some, while others will need a real turnaround. It's not going to happen overnight. Imagine your mind as a huge articulated lorry that's been travelling in one direction but needs to turn round and go another way. It can't just spin round or do a neat three-point turn. It's going to take time, care and a lot of space and so will your mind.

Be gentle and understanding in this as in every aspect of your recovery; offer what you can do to God and ask him to help you with the next stage.

14

Shaping the future –
protecting ourselves

As we saw in the last two chapters, part of our work towards preventing another episode of depression may involve engaging more fully with our past, including the memories, thoughts and emotions that are still causing us problems.

We also need to look to the future and find ways of caring for ourselves that strike a realistic balance between being over-cautious in what we do on the one hand and reckless as to the demands we make of ourselves on the other.

If we wrap ourselves up too much in cotton wool and never move out of our comfort zone (which isn't a large area when we're depressed!) we will never learn or grow in mind and spirit and our lives will be self-limiting. But if we throw ourselves into the crazy hectic lifestyles that so many people seem to lead (and perhaps we ourselves once led) we risk another huge crash and yet more time in the 'A&E' days of recovery.

Once again, we have to find our own ways of looking after ourselves and deciding what we can and can't do, but I'd like to offer here some guidelines which, from my own experience and the experience of other people I've talked to, may help as you seek your way forward, remembering always that the God whose name is 'I AM' will be with you every step along the way.

Emergency strategy

I wrote earlier about having recently experienced an unwelcome dip into depression. It must have been building up for some time but either I wasn't alert enough to catch the warning signs or I didn't do enough to prevent myself going further down. I've realized over the years that unfortunately once we begin to descend into that dark pit we can also begin to lose the ability to see what's happening. It's all too easy to fall back into unhelpful patterns of thought and behaviour and to allow our emotional state to overwhelm us. Before we know it we're sinking quite quickly and need 'emergency' treatment to bring us up out of the gloom.

I think it's a good idea to plan ahead and have an 'emergency strategy' in place, like a lifebelt beside a river. The hope is that we never need to use it but it could make a big difference to our recovery if we do find ourselves up to the neck in troubled waters.

Adrian and I call this the stage when we need to 'treat the illness' rather than look for solutions to whatever issues may have contributed to the dip.

This is the stage when some of the symptoms we've experienced during an episode of depression start reappearing in a way that begins to disrupt our lives again. Each of us will know what our symptoms are. For me, the early morning waking, with feelings of dread, high anxiety or hopelessness, is always the first to appear and the last to go. Actually it's a symptom that rarely goes away completely but when I'm well it's rarely anywhere near enough to make it a struggle for me to begin the day.

My emergency strategy for treating the illness is as follows.

- Write down my commitments in terms of meetings, duties that require prior preparation such as preaching and writing deadlines, social arrangements and so on.
- Do a reality check on how much there is that I really have to do and how much can be readily postponed or cancelled. Sometimes this is enough to reduce my anxiety levels sufficiently to allow me to cope with everything because there isn't actually as much pressure as I feared.
- Decide, if I do need to take a break, on a length of time without those sorts of commitments so that I can recover and regain some mental energy.
- Enlist the help, support and prayers of colleagues and friends who understand my need to do this.
- Try to rest and relax as much as possible *without feeling guilty*!

I am so blessed in having friends and colleagues around me who understand that occasionally I need to activate this strategy and are willing to take on duties and support me through a wobbly phase.

I think it's worth taking time to work out what you can do if you feel you're in danger of sinking down again. This may be very difficult if you have to care for children, elderly parents or have other responsibilities that cannot be taken on by others. But if you can find some way of allowing yourself time and space to recharge your batteries this may well prevent things getting to a crisis point.

This may be the right place to suggest ways in which churches can support members of their congregations who are struggling with depression or other difficulties in their lives.

Pastoral care and support, prayer and compassionate understanding are all important for anyone going through a rough time of any kind and may be offered both informally by friends and more formally by pastoral assistants, clergy and other lay ministers. But I'd encourage churches also to be aware of people who are willing to help others through a rocky patch in very practical ways. For example, there may be those who would be happy to do some washing and ironing; help with lifts to appointments; do some shopping; cook one family meal a week that can just be heated up or kept in the freezer; mow a lawn and do other gardening jobs; look after young children or sit with an elderly parent for a while. This kind of practical support can make a huge difference especially for people with families to care for.

Prevention is better than cure

Having put in place an emergency strategy for times when depression seems to be building up again, we can turn our attention towards preventing it ever being needed!

I've found that for me the key to prevention lies in developing my self-awareness and monitoring my state of mind and emotional reactions to people and events. We need to watch out for and pay attention to the warning signs that may mean that things are not as they should be.

Jane, whose bottled-up anger was causing her problems, noticed that when she was feeling under pressure her anger would start coming up to the surface. Things she'd normally find annoying anyway (for example, a door near her office that was often left to slam shut) would become unbearable and would trigger a fury that would erupt when she could no longer contain it. Jane recognized her fury and feelings of powerlessness, which came from her much younger self, and was able to do a 'reality check'. She asked herself, 'Am I powerless now in the face of what is making me angry?' She learned that if she was not powerless she could take some sort of action for herself, and if she was unable to do anything about the cause of her anger she could choose to let that anger go and accept, maybe not with serenity, the situation as it was.

Sally made a connection between the harm done to her during her childhood and her need as an adult to protect her 'personal space'. She learned to notice when being among other people – on a bus, perhaps, or in a lift or a busy shop – caused her anxiety to increase to a level of panic. That for her was a warning that she needed to create space for herself to breathe more easily and think about what might be behind this increased sensitivity. She learned that having done this she could, for example, choose to walk part of a journey rather than taking a bus for the whole of it, thus regaining a sense of her personal space.

Sometimes other people may notice that we are 'not ourselves' and are perhaps beginning to struggle. Adrian notices that my breathing changes and he picks up the 'vibes' that I'm feeling low. We may have friends who know our warning signs and we might ask them to tell us if they're concerned about our state of mind. I've found that this can be very helpful, especially when friends notice a pattern that I myself hadn't spotted. I can then work out what I need to do to build myself up again.

It might also be an idea to 'check in' with our GP from time to time. During my recent 'dip' I was aware that the main symptom causing me problems was high anxiety. I was finding it hard to relax mentally and wasn't sleeping that well. I discussed this with my doctor, who pre-scribed a different antidepressant designed to treat anxiety. Fortunately I was able to use my current antidepressant alongside the new one during this transition so there was no major disruption to my medica-tion. My anxiety levels did indeed reduce and that helped to lift me up out of the dip.

There are frequently new drugs coming into use and if a certain symptom or side effect is particularly troubling it may be worth asking about the possibility of alternative treatment. Having said that, a change to new medication isn't always as straightforward as my transition was, and this would need to be discussed with our GP, who can advise on the pros and cons of any such alteration in our treatment.

The bruised reed

While I've been writing about planning an emergency strategy and taking preventative steps to keep depression at bay, I've been aware that some of the suggestions I've made, especially about our need for time and space to recover, may seem unrealistic, possibly self-indulgent or 'over the top'. Certainly there have been times in the past when I've felt misunderstood and judged in that sort of way. I've also met people who tell me about their own experience, saying things like:

- 'I feel so pathetic not being able to cope with as much as I used to.'
- 'I feel I'm letting other people down.'
- 'I feel like I'm making a fuss over nothing.'
- 'Everyone else seems to manage all right, why can't I?'

They're all remarks that are hard on the speakers; they are putting themselves down especially in comparison to others.

Once again, this may be something that's hard to understand unless you've been through this experience, but when it comes to depression prevention is most definitely better than cure. And if we don't seek ways of stopping it developing into a major episode our illness will be far more disruptive to our lives and to the lives of others than any preventative measures we put in place for ourselves.

Living a life overwhelmed by anxiety, stress, deep sadness and physical debilitation is not what God wants for any of us, and Jesus came that we might have and enjoy life in all its abundance.

So I think we do need to be kind to ourselves, with the gentle compassion of God who will not break a bruised reed or quench a dimly burning wick (Isaiah 42.1–3).

15

Shaping the future – forgiveness

In this chapter we're going to be reflecting on the huge issue of for-giveness. Because this is such a vast subject I'm focusing here on forgiveness in relation to the 'hidden things' that might lie behind depression and which we've been talking about in this book. Having said that, I hope these reflections may have something to offer others too.

Christian teaching

When we set out to explore the journey of recovering from depression we spent some time thinking about what we meant by 'recovery' and I'd like to do the same as we think about forgiveness. I think this is really important for us as Christians because Jesus is very clear indeed about our need to be forgiving and to be forgiven:

- He teaches us to pray 'Our Father in heaven . . . forgive us our sins as we forgive those who sin against us.'
- He tells us a story about a man who threatens and imprisons someone who owes him a small amount of money even though he himself has been released from a truly crippling debt which he had no hope of settling. This man's refusal to release his own debtor takes from him the freedom he was given. It imprisons him, brings 'torture' upon him and requires him now to pay back that impossibly huge sum of money (Matt. 18.23–30).

In both these teachings Jesus is saying that God's mercy and forgive-ness can only be poured out on us if we allow it to flow through us to other people, to those who hurt us. If we block that flow by refusing to forgive others then we will no longer be able to receive God's gift. At the end of the story in Matthew Jesus says 'so my heavenly Father will also do to every one of you, if you do not forgive your brother or sister *from your heart*' (Matt. 18.35).

I don't know about you but that ending frightens me because there are many, many times when for various reasons I feel I can't or won't forgive from my heart someone who has done me harm. I've reflected a lot about this and would like to share with you some of my thoughts in the hope that they may be helpful if you also struggle with the whole issue of forgiveness and faith.

A defining moment

Once, after a long discussion with a friend about forgiveness, I felt I needed to look up a dictionary definition of the verb 'to forgive' and found this: 'to cease to blame or hold resentment against'. Reading those words gave me a moment of clarity and insight that changed the way I thought about forgiveness and set me off on a path that is still leading me into a deeper understanding of this complex process.

I'd like to set my thoughts in the context of Sandra's story and discuss how she might find a way towards forgiving those who had harmed her in her early years and so find a new freedom from the long-term effects of that harm.

Harm done

Sandra's parents had been very critical, judgemental and unpredict-able towards her and in their general approach to life. Living in this atmosphere inevitably affected Sandra's emotional development. She grew up with low self-esteem and little self-confidence. She was a perfectionist, wanting always to get things right and win approval. She had difficulty forming healthy relationships and was in an almost constant state of anxiety because she was never sure what might happen next in any given situation. Over the years she had built up a great deal of anger and resentment, which in turn led to further problems including episodes of depression.

We've seen how Sandra was able to identify her thoughts and feel-ings, to understand where they came from and to begin the process of integrating her experiences into the present.

Now Sandra faces a challenge in her spiritual life. She knows that she 'must' forgive her parents as well as others who have hurt her over the years. But she can't forgive, not yet, and certainly not 'from the heart'. As the feelings and thoughts of her younger self rise to the surface she feels renewed anger about how she was treated and a strong sense of injustices that need to be put right. How can she forgive, feeling as she does at the moment?

If we are at this stage in our recovery it may be that all we can say is that we cannot forgive and even find it difficult to want to forgive, but that we are willing to seek ways forward with God's help and guidance.

What forgiveness isn't

Let's look again at my dictionary's definition of 'to forgive': 'to cease to blame or hold resentment against'.

Forgiving, for Sandra, does not mean thinking or saying that the way she was treated was all right or that the harm done to her doesn't matter. She will not be asked to deny her experiences or belittle her own feelings.

If she forgives, Sandra does not have to let people continue hurting her and she does not have to trust them in the future. Forgiveness is not about allowing hurtful behaviour to continue unchallenged.

It's also not about trying to forget that the hurtful things were ever said or done. Sandra may well remain vulnerable to hurt when other people's words or actions trigger memories and touch still sensitive wounds. It will be important that Sandra is aware of this so that she can look after herself and avoid getting caught up in a spiralling build-up of hurt, anger and resentment.

So what is forgiveness?

I have no definitive answer to this question, but offer here my thoughts on some of the issues that may be involved in forgiving others on our journey of recovery.

Understanding the harm done

I sense that we need to have an understanding of the nature of our wounds. This might seem a strange thing to say but it may not always be clear to us how we have been harmed and how that harm has affected us over the years.

Sandra has come to understand that her distorted view of herself, which developed from her early experiences, led to various difficulties in her life: she consistently underachieved at school and didn't go on to higher education; she found relationships with colleagues very difficult and was unable to settle into any job or develop a career plan; her frequent episodes of depression caused problems for her at work (including the number of days she took as sick leave) and within all her relationships; her insecurity and need for approval led her into potentially risky relationships with men, and on one occasion she was bullied into handing over a significant sum of money.

Our stories may be very different from Sandra's but it's possible that we, like her, may need to understand the extent of the harm done to us so that we can grasp the reality of what we are being asked to forgive.

Understanding the people

I think that most, if not all, of the harm done to our minds, our emotions and our ways of relating to others takes place within relationships, and the chances are that those relationships have always been with other people who to a greater or lesser extent have also been damaged by their own experiences.

As Sandra develops a greater understanding of the relationships and experiences of members of her family and the ways in which individuals were themselves harmed she is able to get a wider perspective on how it came about that she was treated as she was.

This in turn leads to her having a better understanding of where responsibility for the harm done to her may lie. She can see more clearly where her forgiveness would be needed if she was 'to cease to blame or hold resentment against' those who had hurt her in the past, whether it was in thought, word or deed and whether it was through negligence, weakness or deliberate fault.

Forgiving ourselves

It's perhaps inevitable that sometimes, maybe even most of the time, we will blame ourselves for things that have happened in the past and direct our anger inwards. Sandra berated herself frequently during sessions with her counsellor for being, as she now saw it, stupid enough to believe the man who robbed her of a large sum of money which she had saved up to use as a deposit on a house she was hoping to buy.

With her counsellor's help Sandra came to understand why, given her past experiences and need for love, she had been so vulnerable and willing to do what this man wanted when he said that he loved her and was committed to their relationship.

We may regret many things we have done in the past and it's easy with hindsight to tell ourselves we should have done things differently. I think that we often need to be kinder to ourselves and understand why we behaved as we did. We need to dispel that anger we're directing into ourselves and forgive the person we were then, resolving to do things differently from now on. And it's this resolution that will begin to shape our future and lead us further into recovery.

Victim no more

In the early stages of a severe episode of depression Sandra felt overwhelmed by the illness and unable to deal with the 'hidden things' that lay behind it. She felt like a victim, held captive by the past in ways she didn't fully understand and over which she felt powerless, unable to see a way forward into the future.

In time Sandra begins to reach a deeper understanding of her own story, her thoughts and feelings and how she had become who she was when she fell ill. She then begins to realize that with that understanding comes responsibility and the ability to make choices about the future. She can now choose to break old patterns of thoughts and feelings; she doesn't have to be held captive by them any more.

She also realizes that part of breaking those old patterns would be to forgive those who had harmed her in the past – to stop blaming them and holding resentment against them, because that blaming, resentment and anger are harming her in the present and were part of her serious illness.

In forgiving the people who first harmed her and letting go of her anger and resentment, Sandra is able to rebuild and make new relationships without all that emotional 'baggage' getting in the way. Sandra is no longer a victim of her past as she learns to take responsibility for her future, to shape it herself by forgiving the people and letting go of the destructive feelings that had held her captive.

The power of forgiveness

Forgiveness is very powerful and can change lives. It takes commitment and courage and a willingness to be very honest about our own thoughts and feelings. And it is a process, I believe, that will continue throughout our lives. We may find that we have to forgive, to cease blaming and resenting, the same person many times for the same harm they have done, but the fact that we are committed to the road of forgiveness is surely enough for God who understands how hard and costly that road can be.

Some final thoughts on forgiveness

As I said earlier, forgiveness is a huge issue with special importance for Christians and I have barely scratched the surface of all that is involved. I'd like to recommend reading the very sensitive chapter on forgiveness in Andrew and Elizabeth Procter's excellent book *Encountering Depression: Frequently asked questions answered for Christians.*[7]

And I'd like also just to outline one or two areas I haven't mentioned in this chapter, which may well be part of our struggle with forgiveness.

- We may need to make decisions about what we say to the people involved in our story whom we are learning to forgive. Sometimes it may be possible to talk through issues with them and reach an understanding together of what has happened in the past and how to go forward into the future.
- The people we feel we need to forgive may not be aware of any harm they have done or may not be able to acknowledge that harm as their responsibility.
- The people who have harmed us may no longer be alive, which can make it difficult for us to hold them responsible and then to forgive them.
- There are some things that just seem unforgivable and the harm goes very deep inside us. We cannot forgive to order and it may take a long, long time to get to a point where we can even consider it as a possibility.
- We have the assurance of God's forgiveness for us for the things we have done wrong 'through ignorance, through weakness, through our own deliberate fault'. God has set us free from the burden of our wrongdoing and wants us to play our part in setting other people free from their burdens too.
- Holding on to anger, hatred, blaming, resentment and all sorts of negativity weighs us down and depresses us. Although aimed against someone else these things, in the end, hurt only us. Forgiving others frees us from their clutches. It is a life-giving way which leads towards the recovery in body, mind and spirit that we so want and need for ourselves.

Part 5

JOYS AND SORROWS

16

Sorrow and sighing

———•◦•———

Two boys are running along the top of quite a high wall. Suddenly they both slip, lose their balance and fall. One boy suffers some nasty cuts and bruises and is clearly shaken up. The other boy hits his head when he lands and his leg is badly twisted under him. The first boy's injuries and shock require attention and treatment but this can be given at home by Mum. The second boy, though, needs different care. An ambulance is called and the paramedics assess the boy's injuries before taking him to hospital. His leg is fractured and he's also kept under close observation because of the head wound, which has needed stitches.

The two boys have had accidents that could be described in the same words – 'He fell off a wall' – but the outcome and subsequent treatment of each boy is different.

In this chapter we're going to be thinking about some experiences of loss and bereavement and the feelings of grief that follow them. These experiences and feelings are shared by all of us, as they are woven into our lives as human beings. There will be differences, though, in the nature of the losses we suffer and in the ways we are affected by those losses, just as the two boys were affected differently when they fell off the wall. One of those differences may be the part depression is playing in both our loss and our grief.

Depression and grief

Depression often brings with it a deep sense of loss and grief, although it may not always be clear what has been lost or what is behind that grief. These feelings of deep sadness may lift with a period of rest and recovery and/or as the depression is treated with medication. But very often there is more to it than that and, as we've seen, what lies beneath the surface may be complex, requiring time and patience to unwrap and understand.

Using the stories of the people we've already met in this book, let's have a look at some of the things we may be grieving for when we're depressed and recovering from that illness.

- Peter and Jane both became aware of how many of their friendships had been affected or broken by their tendency to become angry and resentful when they felt let down or hurt by people they had trusted. They needed to grieve for those losses and, as can happen when someone is grieving following a bereavement, they also experienced deep regret and guilt for some of the things they said and did, which cannot now be put right.
- Sandra deeply regretted not having gone to university, although she knew that at the time she wouldn't have been able to cope with it emotionally. She also regretted not having had the confidence to take up an opportunity once offered for training, which would have led to a potentially very rewarding professional career. In her life there were many questions about 'what might have been' and she needed to grieve for the missed opportunities and unknown alternative paths she could have followed.
- Sandra and Sally both experienced a deep sense of loss about the childhood they didn't have, and felt this acutely when they saw the close and happy relationships enjoyed within other families.
- For James the depression he experienced was so severe that he was unable to return to his job with a firm who couldn't offer him any alternative work or adjust his hours. Thus depression itself caused the loss of a very important part of James's life – a job that he found fulfilling with a more than adequate salary and colleagues whose company he enjoyed.

Because of the circumstances of their lives, Peter, Jane, Sandra, James and Sally may have been carrying around within them a heavy burden of suppressed grief, perhaps not even realizing it was there. This pent-up grief, like suppressed anger and fear, can itself be among the causes of depression. Recovery for all of them may involve being able to identify and understand their grief and then somehow expressing their feelings safely before letting go of the losses behind the grief. Each will have to find their own way of doing this, as will we if we recognize our own need to grieve for losses and regrets in our own lives.

Bereavement, loss and recovery

Depression can descend upon us as part of a process of grieving after some sort of bereavement or loss. That's not to say that these circumstances make it any easier to cope with or to recover from. But it may make it more understandable to people looking on who will perhaps be able to identify with what someone is going through. These might be the major losses of the death of someone we love or the break-up of a special relationship. Each of these has its own unique characteristics and perhaps only those who have been through such experiences can fully appreciate the particular pain and grief they bring.

What may not be as easily understood is that there are many other losses we might experience that can trigger a sense of bereavement, grief and an episode of depression.

- Very often parents grieve as their children leave home. It's the ending of one stage in life, which brings big changes for everyone involved including the brothers and sisters of the one who has moved on.
- Retirement might unexpectedly trigger depression when someone experiences a loss of identity and purpose and misses the daily routines and contact with other people.
- Health problems or injury may mean having to give up some activity or sport and there may be a sense of grief around the loss of hopes, dreams and ambitions as well as the loss of enjoyment of the activity itself.
- Moving house is known to be one of the most stressful events in people's lives. Even if the move is to an area in which we've chosen to live and for good reasons, we can still experience a sense of loss when we leave what was familiar to us. We need a period of adjustment and settling in and in that time of transition we may be vulnerable to a sense of grief and depression.

I think what I'm trying to say is that major changes in our lives, even ones for the better, can trigger a sense of loss and bereavement that can then lead to an episode of depression. So if we find ourselves going back down into the depths at any time in our journey of recovery, it might be worth thinking about any changes that have taken place in our lives that might be behind the dip.

If we can identify some such change in our lives it may help us to grieve for that particular loss in a healthy way without going too far down into depression. This is all part of looking after ourselves and recognizing our own particular vulnerabilities.

'Jesus wept'

The shortest verse in the Bible (John 11.35, REB), but packed with meaning. Jesus knows about grief. He witnesses it in so many other people: anxious and distressed parents, brothers, sisters, friends, even employers all desperate for someone they love to be healed, or even brought back to life from the brink of death. On this occasion, in John 11, he witnesses the grief of two of his close friends, Mary and Martha, whose brother has died. And he experiences the grief in his own heart over the death of Lazarus. Jesus is indeed 'a man of suffering and acquainted with infirmity' and he promises to be with us always.

I wonder if perhaps we are at our most childlike when our grief overwhelms us, and that emptiness that is loss opens up inside us. If so, maybe it's then that we are closest to the tender loving heart of God who longs to wipe away our tears (healing as tears can be) and bring us new hope even in that dark empty place of loss, just as he brought Easter resurrection and joy out of the darkness and pain of Good Friday.

17

Joy and gladness

The ransomed of the Lord shall return with singing,
with everlasting joy upon their heads.

Joy and gladness shall be theirs,
and sorrow and sighing shall flee away.
('A Song of the Wilderness', *CWDP*, p. 580)

Redemption

Depression is a terrible illness. It's destructive and cruel. Its presence reaches out beyond its victim to darken the lives of people close by. Once experienced, it can exercise power by the threat of its return and there is nothing remotely good about what it does to those in its grip.

I do not for one minute believe that God deliberately puts any of us, his children, through this dreadful experience any more than he deliberately causes any other forms of life-changing or life-threatening illness.

What I do believe passionately, from my own experience and from what I've seen happen in other people's lives, is that even in the most wretched of places and out of the darkest imaginable pain God can and does bring healing, beauty and joy, strength and peace. He redeems our suffering by giving it meaning and turning it into a source of goodness.

Recovery

Clinical depression

Recovering from clinical depression can be a very slow and long-drawn-out process. It may take a while to find the right kind of medication, whether we're using conventional or complementary treatments. Even the right remedies might take some time to be effective and longer still to bring us to a point where the symptoms of the illness no longer overwhelm us.

These early days are tough and distressing both for the person affected and for those who love and care for him or her. If we can, depressed person and carers alike need to hang on to a belief that this dreadful phase will pass and life will become less heavy, dark and hopeless. It will help if we can also place some faith in 'that of God' within us which is always working to bring us new life and hope, sometimes in the face of apparently insurmountable difficulties.

At some point our doctors (or other health practitioners) may advise on a longer-term prognosis for our illness and whether or not we will need to continue with treatment. Again this may be something that can only be assessed over a long period of time with close monitoring of our symptoms.

Eventually, though, we will find a degree of stability in our condition that allows us to live our lives free of the worst symptoms and no longer mentally paralysed by the effects of clinical depression.

The hidden things

Recovering from the hidden things that may have contributed to our depression can also be a very slow and long-drawn-out process. In Chapter 6 I talked about 'some essentials' that will be needed on this journey of recovery: courage, motivation, determination, commitment, a sense of personal responsibility and loving-kindness towards ourselves.

This would be a daunting list for anyone but for someone worn out, weak and vulnerable, struggling in the depths of depression, it will seem, and almost certainly will be, impossible to summon up.

Paying attention to and working on these hidden things is not something to be undertaken during the early days of recovery from clinical depression. What we can do quite early on, though, is think about what was happening in our lives in the weeks or months leading up to the diagnosis. This may give us an idea of the issues we will probably need to address when we are stronger. So, for example, in Chapter 2 I outlined some of the hidden things lying behind the depression I experienced in 1999: deep dissatisfaction but 'stuckness' in my working life, bereavement, and long-term emotional difficulties.

I was aware of all these things lurking in the background but it was some time before I could begin to work with them and to form a new relationship with each of them, which has allowed me to free myself from the grip they had over me.

We will probably find that progress in this area of recovery is neither linear nor at a steady pace. We may well revisit various issues but at different levels – on a spiral rather than round in flat circles. We may go for long periods of time without being troubled by any of them, then for some reason one of them makes its presence felt again and we find we need to do a little more work on it. This has been my experience but I've also found that that work gets easier the more I've learnt about it up to that point.

As with clinical depression, I believe that we can reach a degree of stability on this inner journey of recovery that allows us to enjoy lives no longer held captive by the past.

Back to normal

Do our lives ever get back to normal after an episode of clinical depression? Well, it depends what we mean by 'normal'!

From my personal experience, and again from the experiences of other people I've spoken with, our lives are changed and reshaped by depression. Life cannot be as it was 'Before the Darkness'. Sometimes that's because it was a major change in our lives that triggered the depression: a significant bereavement, the loss of a job, a serious illness. Sometimes it's because living through an episode of depression has either forced us to make big changes in our lives or prompted us to choose to make such changes.

Jesus says, 'no one puts new wine into old wineskins; otherwise the new wine will burst the skins and will be spilled, and the skins will be destroyed. But new wine must be put into fresh wineskins' (Luke 5.37–38). In the early days of our recovery we may well learn many things about ourselves that we cannot unlearn, and come to see life in new ways that we cannot then ignore. The old wineskin of the life we lived before depression descended probably won't be the same as the new wineskin of the life we are going to live after it.

In that sense our lives will probably not go back to what used to be normal for us. However, we may find that we are living a life that might be described as 'normal' for people who have not experienced depression. In other words we will have ups and downs, good days and bad days, hopes and fears, joys and sorrows – all the things that make us human but without the extreme darkness, heavy weight and hopelessness that depression brings with it. Like everyone else we will have our vulnerabilities, and one of those will probably be a tendency to depression but that need not overwhelm us or prevent us from living our new life to the full.

And the new life that grows from our period in the wilderness, the new thing that God is doing for us, can be exciting, fruitful and hope-filled.

The new things

Emotions

As we've followed the stories of Sally, Peter, Jane, James and Sandra through this book we've seen how they were all troubled by very strong but bottled-up and suppressed emotions: anger, fear, hatred, grief and so on. As they talked with therapist, counsellor or spiritual guide they each came to understand why they felt as they did and learned how to release and let go of these emotions in ways that were safe for them and for others.

As the top came off the bottle and all the negativity began dispersing something happened that they hadn't expected. They found that in suppressing all those powerful and scary emotions they had also been suppressing joyful and life-enhancing emotions. It happened gradually, but they began to enjoy good things in life in a new way. Their delight in seeing and hearing beautiful things seemed clearer and sharper; happiness at being with people they loved seemed deeper and stronger and love itself blossomed with new tenderness and joy.

Sadness, anger or fear can still be stirred up, as they can in everyone, but now they are more straightforward emotions uncomplicated by shadows of the unknown and from the past.

Buried treasure

James rediscovered in himself a love for music that had been almost suffocated by his avoidance of the raw emotions it could stir up. He joined a choral group and his singing brought him a deep sense of fulfilment and pleasure.

Sally continued to develop her artistic gifts and began producing greetings cards with both spiritual and secular designs which she started selling locally in shops and at events like craft fairs and fêtes.

Sandra developed an interest in psychology and decided to study for the degree she missed out on by not going to university.

Peter got involved in a charity dedicated to supporting people in mental distress or ill health. He became a compassionate and effective advocate for people struggling to cope with the practical difficulties presented by their particular circumstances.

Jane undertook a course on aspects of Christian spirituality and found that increasingly people sought her guidance and support for their own spiritual journey and in their relationship with God.

And for these people, underpinning each new venture, was a deep awareness of the precious gift of life, the priceless value of love and friendships and the way in which we can support one another through good times and bad with the God who is 'I AM', holding us all together in his love and the light that the darkness can never overcome.

18

Some final thoughts

------◆•◆------

I would much rather not have had to experience such frequent episodes of depression over so many years and I still have questions I want to, and do, ask God about. But I've learnt that I have a choice about how I view this. I can continue to regret that it took so long for me to reach a place where depression no longer shapes my life. Or I can be thankful and glad that I have reached that place and am finding an enjoyment and delight in life that I had not thought possible. I pray that with God's help I will continue, day by day, to choose the latter approach.

Several times while I've been writing this book I've stopped and reminded myself to listen to my own advice! Sometimes I run into difficulties because I've got overtired or over-committed. Sometimes I've once more felt overwhelmed by my own emotions or the pressure I feel I'm under (often self-imposed). And sometimes I feel over-responsible for other people's welfare. But for me recovery has been, and probably will continue to be, about becoming aware of my own limitations and learning to live within those limitations, with occasional quick forays to see if they've stretched a bit!

I do believe that I have been following a God-given sense of vocation to write in his service and I hope that in sharing my experience of living with depression and moving forward on the road towards recovery I may be offering support and companionship to others on similar journeys. I believe that is how God is redeeming my time in the wilderness and for that I am deeply and eternally grateful.

I wish you well on your journey, wherever it's taking you.

> May the Lord bless you and watch over you,
> may he make his face shine upon you
> and be gracious to you,
> may the Lord look kindly on you
> and give you his peace now and always. Amen.
> (Adapted from Num. 6.24–26)

Notes

1 J. K. Rowling, *Harry Potter and the Prisoner of Azkaban* (London: Bloomsbury, 1999), Chapter 10.
2 *Common Worship: Additional Collects* (London: The Archbishops' Council, 2004), p. 10.
3 Reinhold Niebuhr, 1892–1971.
4 L. M. Willis, 1824–1908.
5 Collegeville, MN: Liturgical Press, 1989.
6 *Common Worship: Times and Seasons* (London: The Archbishops' Council, 2006), p. 335.
7 London: SPCK, 2012.

Suggestions for further reading

We all have individual preferences about our leisure reading so we will also have preferences when it comes to books about recovery. But finding the right book for ourselves is not easy – where do we start looking? There is a bewildering choice available dealing with depression, anxiety, difficulties in relationships and every other field of personal growth we can think of. And there are just as many books about our spiritual life and growth.

Personal recommendations sometimes prove helpful so I'm going to suggest just a few books that might offer helpful insights and suggestions to others.

Andrew and Elizabeth Procter, *Encountering Depression: Frequently asked questions answered for Christians* (London: SPCK, 2012). This is an excellent book full of information, helpful suggestions and guidance. It is compassionate in its approach and recognizes the particular difficulties Christians might face when suffering from depression. It's realistic about how things might be and doesn't use words like 'should' and 'ought'!

Katharine Smith, *Angels in the Wilderness: Hope and healing in depression* (Alton: Redemptorist Publications, 2010). When I set out to write this book I wanted it to be the sort of book I would have found helpful in the darkest days of depression and the earliest days of recovery. I particularly wanted to 'reframe' some of the Gospel stories in the light of my experiences of depression and my struggles with faith when it seemed that God either couldn't or wouldn't reach me and heal me.

Brian C. Taylor, *Spirituality for Everyday Living: An adaptation of the Rule of St Benedict* (Collegeville, MN: Liturgical Press, 1989). A very simple and helpful guide to building up our spiritual life around our day-to-day living.

Alan Jamieson, *Journeying in Faith: In and beyond the tough places* (London: SPCK, 2004). As its title suggests, this book explores the experiences of people who have been through some difficult times and have often felt that their church cannot meet their spiritual needs at such times. These are people who have explored faith outside established religion to find a place where they feel accepted as themselves. Those who have found a lack of understanding of depression in the Church may find this a welcome companion.

Tom Wright, *The Crown and the Fire: Meditations on the Cross and the Life of the Spirit* (London: SPCK, 1992). I read the first part of this book during the three weeks I spent as a voluntary patient in a psychiatric unit. It was during Lent and this seemed like suitable reading. I remember deriving a great comfort from these meditations, which showed me that not even the Son of God could escape suffering and he could understand what I was going through at that time.

Paul Gilbert, *Overcoming Depression: A self-help guide using Cognitive Behavioural Techniques* (London: Constable and Robinson, 3rd edition, 2009). This is a weighty volume and I use it as a reference book to dip into. It's well written in clear language with no mystifying jargon and is practical as well as theoretical. The first part discusses the causes of depression and contributing factors such as evolution, chemistry, genetics and early life experiences. It deals extensively with what I've called the 'hidden things' that can lie behind depression, the relationship between thoughts and feelings and how we can learn to change our patterns of thinking and therefore our feelings. It's not a book with easy answers but it'll certainly give you something to get your teeth into on the journey of recovery.

Thomas A. Harris, *I'm OK – You're OK* (London: Arrow Books, 2012, first published in 1973). Forty years on, this book is still a classic. It had a huge impact on me when I first read it in the mid 1980s. It helped me to understand so much more about my ways of relating to people and how I might have learnt those patterns. The book is based on something called Transactional Analysis which seeks to understand how the mind operates, 'why we do what we do, and how we can stop doing what we do if we wish'. It does this by examining the kind of relationships we have or have had with others, particularly in our childhood. The thinking is that once we understand the nature of those relationships, we can choose to change our role within them and take responsibility for how we relate to others in the future. There are therapists who are practitioners in Transactional Analysis and can offer therapy based on the principles described in this book.

Gregory L. Jantz, *Healing the Scars of Emotional Abuse* (New York: Revell, 1995). I would prefer this book to be entitled 'Healing the Scars of Emotional Harm' but I suppose that wouldn't have the same impact! As I discussed in Chapter 6 of this book, while there are people who do set out to abuse others and have no concern whatsoever for the welfare of those they hurt, many of us are harmed by others simply because of their own hurts, their lack of self-knowledge and emotional intelligence and inability to understand the impact of their words and actions. Having said that, I found this to be a very helpful book with lots of stories about people's relationships and ways of being that shed light on how we can be harmed emotionally and how that can affect us very deeply. It utterly contradicts the thinking that 'sticks and stones may break my bones but words can never hurt me'!